THE PRIEST AND THE PENDULUM

RECONCILING THE ORDERS
OF MELCHIZEDEK AND AARON

Dennis McNally, SJ

**A Priest, Trained after Vatican II,
Appraises the Premises and Promise
of a Reaffirmation
of Pre-conciliar Priestly Power**

Copyright © 2010 by Dennis McNally

ISBN 978-0-7414-6143-8

Printed in the United States of America

Published September 2010

INFINITY PUBLISHING
1094 New DeHaven Street, Suite 100
West Conshohocken, PA 19428-2713
Toll-free (877) BUY BOOK
Local Phone (610) 941-9999
Fax (610) 941-9959
Info@buybooksontheweb.com
www.buybooksontheweb.com

This book is dedicated to my sisters,
Kerry Ellen Graham and Regina Mary McNally.

Kerry and Jeanie have taught me
so very much about loyalty, tenderness,
and understanding.

They have always understood and helped me
to be more kind and competent
in celebrating the important
Liturgies in the family.

Wedding, Baptism, Communion, and Funeral,
The Sacrament of the Sick,
All had a tangibly human face
because they expected me to be human
while I took the place of privilege,
speaking for the family,
to God!

Acknowledgment

The author expresses gratitude to Dominc Roberti for his diligent and insightful help in the design and production of this book.

Contents

Preface

Reconciling conflicting calls to the priesthood in the hearts and in the history of Aaron and Melchizedek

Research into a field that used to be called "comparative religion" was necessary as part of the background of my doctoral dissertation. It revealed a theme that courses through most organized religions; the systemic realization that we are not perfect has many manifestations in creation myths leading virtually all religions to develop a notion of "ritual purity" and means to achieve it.

Aztec priests were not to bathe or cut their nails, keeping the blood of the holy victims on their own persons. In a vast culture, economically, politically, and spiritually centered in what Cortez thought of as the largest city in the known world, Tenochtitlan, these priests maintained ritual purity in personal filth, while running water flowed into all the households, fostering a great concern for bathing among normal citizens. So this was a ritual purity for the priests maintained for the whole people.

In other religious bodies ritual purity of priests might be maintained by cleanliness; in Hebrew culture, for instance, it certainly includes distance from blood sacrifices, or even the passing of bodily fluids. Hindu religious practice includes even today recognition of the differences between castes. Where and when people bathe matters immensely. Sharia law in various branches of Islam requires execution of those who have defiled the purity of a family, a clan, or a nation. For Nazis and other extreme proponents of national purity, there arose even a religious element in getting rid of those who are different. The extreme position on ritual purity seems to devolve into a notion that sounds something like this: I am *righteous* because I am not like you!

For ancient Hebrews, and thus for the whole of the Judaeo-Christian world, there were laws about ritual purity for the priests, the people, foreigners, animals, foods, and clothing, so many relationships to people and things could cause a person to be ritually "unclean" and, therefore, to be shunned or stoned.

The call to holiness for a people gets mired in blood, often enough. The violent protection of the purity of the people gets enshrined in books of law for so many religious peoples. I can remember my own mother getting "churched" after the births of my sisters; I wondered what that was all about and only much later discovered that there was a ritual purity requirement in the Church of old by which women had to be purified after the unclean activity associated with childbirth. Something like this happens still in many places.

The bishops of Nigeria, when the colonial regime of the British was retired, allowing blacks and whites to attend services together, recommended that the black Catholics stay at the back of the churches and receive communion later than their "guests." Similarly, when the archbishop of New Orleans, having to deal with the desegregation of the churches in the American South during the drive for civil rights for all citizens, recommended that blacks attend liturgy in the balconies to maintain some respect for the feelings of those who could not tolerate the mixing of the races.

Presently homosexual men and women and those who are genetically or chromosomally both, even though recognized by a vast array of scientific investigation as established in their sexuality by birth (or "nature") rather than by choice (or "nurture"), must be tolerated in the Catholic Church, according to episcopal decrees, but must not exercise their drive to physical intimacy, because the drive itself is seen as "disordered" or unclean. Still there is this drive to establish ritual purity according to a narrow understanding of how I am righteous because I am not you.

The pain and suffering which arises for the unapproved under all these legal codes is undeniable. The desire for order in our world includes this kind of exclusion, doesn't it? The Lord Jesus, however, in so many places acted in a way which allowed Him to deal with sinners while not approving of their sins; but He did not seem to approve of violent restrictions on the internal integrity of the human person. He described the Law in a quite reductionist mode when He answered questions about the Decalogue and all the developed law codes of the Hebrew world. He said the law and the prophets come down to this one idea: Love God with your whole heart, your whole mind, your whole soul, and your whole strength;—and the second is like it: Love your neighbor as yourself.

This comprehension of just what all religious law is about is mind-boggling! In our understanding of what it means for the priest to be ritually pure it becomes transformational. The idea that priesthood itself depends on the ritual purity of the priest resides in legal conceptions of Levitican, Deuteronomical, and Ecclesiastican codes. The priests of Aaron and Levi must wear certain things, must refrain from certain things at certain times, must be removed from office for certain offenses, etc. But the priesthood of Christ, as we see in the *Epistle to the Hebrews*, is the only priesthood; it is the priesthood of Melchizedek, and by His sacrifice are we all saved. I am righteous because I am His. This is completely at odds with the other ways of evaluating righteousness. So the priesthood of Melchizedek becomes something I want to understand better.

Prelude: A Sense of Call

In an article in the *National Catholic Reporter,* Sr. Joan Chitester, O.S.B. (NCR September 2007) writes of the return of a universal right to the Tridentine Rite for Catholic celebration of the liturgy. She sees it as a real threat to advances in ecclesiology, which had been elevated to the level of universal Church praxis by the decisions of the Second Vatican Council concerning the nature of ritual within the Roman Catholic Church. The difficulty as she sees it includes some affronts in the Holy Week liturgies to the *unchurched,* particularly to people of Jewish ancestry. She also sees the return of relegation of the status of women to that of bystander and observer as a danger inherent in this explicit attempt to make the more conservative laity comfortable. My own appreciation of priesthood, informed by an understanding clearly discussed by the writer of the *Epistle to the Hebrews,* as participation in the Priesthood of Melchizedek, is presently in danger of becoming no longer of a principal stand-in, presiding in the ritual role, focusing this priesthood of Christ among the people. It becomes more like the Priesthood of Aaron, with rights and privileges galore, including the central dramatic position at the more mysterious and, perhaps, more elegant Tridentine Rite of Pius V. Here the priest has a more holy, less tangible, and inviolable place within the People of God; he is not so much a substitute for the real thing, he is the real thing!

In the course of my own human events, I have found a vocation. Really rather early on I felt myself motivated to become a priest. In the earliest stages of conscious choice-making, in curious fact, I found myself wanting to be more like the sisters in the convent than like the diocesan clergy in the rectory; I felt that their gift of self was more complete somehow—and besides I liked the flowing elegance of the long black robes! I found myself "called" to what seemed to me a more complete offering, an emptying into the priesthood of Christ. The "call," as it is so often called, comes wrapped in so many indecipherable motivations. But, no doubt about it, there was a very early interest in the things of religion and the subtle but commandingly romantic ideal of absolute commitment to it, to furthering Christ's work.

Therein lies an essential polarity in my own earliest sense of being called. I found a sense of God, a friend, the holiest Christ, the tender, wise, self-sacrificing very image of a divine hero who loved me and who would be my friend and who asked me to follow Him. I was five, sure, and secure, but I felt that, if this is true, then there is nothing to do but to enter fully into it. What was the *this?* The Lord Whom I met in communion and in prayer was It. My whole adult life has been lived almost totally in the comfort of clarity on this point. It is a double-edged reality, because my sense of the real outside of it is based on an experience of it—on the inside. There have, of course, been times of self-doubt and times too of intellectual doubt about the very possibility of such a divinity actually existing, or of His having a Father God, or a Virgin Mother whose humanity is His connection to life as one of us. But I have, so far, always returned in prayer to a more streamlined faith and a stronger realization that the God who made me loves us, that Jesus knows me and loves me. "He walks with me and He talks with me and He tells me I am His own."

The other side of the polarity includes the robes, of course. I found a real liking for the very thought of being part of the "christian empire," of being a royal sort of high priest, someone beyond reproach, someone respected, someone who could do good because he is connected to God Himself. The corollary for this sense of call is that I feel called to serve the Church, the Church which had, in my youth, no public history of abuse or cover-ups. Not until I began to study Roman, Byzantine, or Renaissance history did I ever hear of priests, or nuns for that matter, who were not up to this high calling. I thought there would be some correlation between belonging and being worthy. We tend to conflate appearance and reality, do we not? This was a child's dream, of course worth having, but unrealistic. The realities of church politics and church history have revealed a totally different aspect of the Institution to which I would belong. But belong I do.

So there is a conflict that I found pretty early within myself, between a desire for good order, elegance, and connection and, contrarily, a growing awareness of and love for the self-emptying God, with Whom I could relate, even in the face of earth's entropy in the necessary diminishment of all things, of all holy things, too.

There is a prodigious amount of biblical evidence that God has a similar sense of conflict in His relationships with Israel. The prophets, *Micah* in chapter 3, *Malachi* in chapter 2, *Hosea* in 1, 4, and 5, all wax poetic over God's anger with the priests who aren't doing their jobs, who aren't shepherding the flock toward God. Third *Isaiah* in chapter 56:10 and 11 says, "Israel's sentinels are blind, they are all without knowledge; they are all silent dogs that cannot bark... The shepherds also have no understanding; they have all turned to their own way, to their own gain, one and all." The New RSV translation of *Jeremiah* has this terrifying threat, "Woe to the shepherds who destroy and scatter the sheep of my pasture! ... It is you who have scattered my flock, and have driven them away, and you have not attended to them. So I will attend to you for your evil doings..." (chapter 23:1ff). Furthermore, in chapter 25:33ff: "Wail, you shepherds, and cry out...for the days of your slaughter have come... Flight shall fail the shepherds, and there shall be no escape for the lords of the flock. Hark! the cry of the shepherds, and the wail of the lords of the flock! For the Lord is despoiling their pasture and the peaceful folds are devastated..."Then *Ezekiel* 34:1ff has it: "Mortal, prophesy against the shepherds of Israel: prophesy and say to them— to the shepherds: Thus says the Lord God: Ah, you shepherds of Israel who have been feeding yourselves...My sheep were scattered, they wandered over all the face of the earth, with no one to search or seek for them. Therefore, you shepherds, hear the word of the Lord: As I live, says the Lord God, because my sheep have become a prey, and my sheep have become food for all the wild animals, since there was no shepherd; and because my shepherds have not searched for my sheep, but the shepherds have fed themselves, and not fed my sheep; therefore you shepherds, hear the word of the Lord: Thus says the Lord God, I am against the shepherds..." The idea that priests can have a lot to answer for becomes quite a reason for practicing the great Old Testament virtue of Fear of the Lord! Indeed, this ritual priesthood is replete with pitfalls for the mere human who cannot but sometimes be self-centered, pompous, greedy. How could I choose this "call"?

The *Exercises of St. Ignatius Loyola* are a necessity for becoming and remaining a member of the Society of Jesus. They became part of my life-long daily ritual. There is in them a constant invitation to get to know Him better, to love Him more, and then to follow Him more closely. The idea that one *can* know God is terrifying in itself because it sounds so arrogant, and to the more logically or analytically inclined, rather incapable of proof or even observation. However, there is great comfort in knowing that there is a tradition, a shared reality, whose definition, though mutable according to the experience of the one making the *Exercises*, is yet comprehensible precisely because of the commonalities in the experience. This kind of mystical tradition is wider than Jesuit history, more inclusive than its strains throughout Judaeo/Christian history—and recognizable in the prayers of and literature about the "mystics" of most religious traditions.

There seems to be truth to the experience of God, the Other, beyond verifiable certitude, Who makes ineffable connections with those whom S/He can reach. I feel a sense that my "vocation" arose within the context of the dialogue with God. There is a way that this sense is a time-honored, constant consideration of the Church. There is, however, a sense of being called by the Church for her service, a call to which the People of God acquiesce (emphatically and ritually in the rite of ordination itself) before the priest is ordained. This second sense of call is heard in the Church as coming from the Church. There are, therefore, in other words, two senses of call and they are really quite different. This book is concerned with attending to both. Understanding, both in my own case, and in my own way, is necessary for living the life, answering both calls while attempting to be a whole human being. This neat trick is necessary for any priest, now or in the future, male, married or not, female, married or not, gay, straight, or ambidextrous!

God calls us all to union. We have ordained priests to help us all. The Holy Spirit will, according to the words of Jesus, be with us to whisper. It is our duty to learn how best to understand the "still, small voice" and to respond with heartfelt and committed risk-taking loyalty. This has meant for the prophets of old that they speak most unpleasant prophecies to God's people. It probably means something similar for some prophets today. Those who hear the word of God must keep it and, if encouraged by God to share it, they must do so, because, if they don't, we all perish. So, how does this impinge on the life of those who are called by the Church to be ordained in the present era?

Vatican I/Vatican II

Born, as should be apparent, before the last ecumenical council, I was a child still when it was convened. The understanding with which we were imbued as student priests was clearly honed during and after the Council itself, with strains of growing momentum in the theory and theological reflection of the decades between World War II and Vatican Council II. I think that much of the understanding of the role of the priest, as articulated at the Council but since learned in practice, has been given substance against the backdrop of the *Constitution on the Church in the Modern World*. That backdrop, colored by discussions of the role of the laity and a ratification of the idea that there is a more widespread call to discipleship, needs further development. But there was a sense of the human vulnerability of all leadership, an awareness that the leadership which ruled the world (and included the Church's hierarchy),is, in this sense,capable of mistakes. That which later history has revealed but which was somewhat more evident to Church professionals with access to the pulse of the curial coxswain, through having cast their oars into ecclesial waters, is a vulnerability carried on the shoulders of politically motivated and oftentimes inattentive human agents. There grew a deep realization that the Church is led by the Holy Spirit, who breathes where She wills, not necessarily in the halls of princely courts, nor onto crowned heads, nor indeed into the will of an elected leader, no matter what manner of anointing they'd experienced. The vocation to priesthood has had a consequentially necessary re-inventive quality. The "priesthood of the laity" comes from a harkening back to the roots of Christianity, priesthood seen through *Romans*, *Hebrews*, a study of the words of the Last Supper, and reflection on the meaning and growth of grace on the surface of human, political, and ecclesial nature.

In my own development as a practicing priest, I have found conflict in the realization of these two contrary calls—on the one hand, the call of the prophet in response to dialogue with God, on the other, the call of the leader of ritual in response to his cultic responsibilities and accountability within the Church. My own studies and prayer had led me to think the two are linked in the Church as two sides of the same coin, but I have found it more, in experience, as two blades on the same sword.

Many of the elders under whom I came up as a priest were trained before the Vatican Council and there was for them a great tearing from tradition in the way that Vatican II "dis-edified" what had become the infrastructure of priesthood. They were part of something old and solid, lasting historically through the "Tridentine Liturgy" of Pius V and in service of it, but emotionally from time immemorial. The contrary calls became, eventually, clarions for differing camps who saw priesthood in two separate and not contrary but contradictory ways. The still small voice became a claxon of contradiction. How could this be!?

Reconciliation (as sought in my own liturgical life)

Herein lies a grounding, at least, for an intellectual battle. The battleground has become bloodied with duels to the death. The conflict of ideologies became the daily porridge of even the lowliest workers in the field. This sounds enough like the prophetic conflicts between father and son, mother-in-law and daughter-in-law, which Jesus envisioned, the promise of the Beatitudes for those who hunger and thirst after justice, for His name's sake, the cup, from which we, too, must drink.

There is still hope that the kingdom can reign in the hearts and be felt on the real flesh of the human community; that the battles for dominance might cease because the heart of Christ is beating in the breast of the Church; that, in peace, we might go out from the worshiping Church, carrying our sheaves. Two ways of looking at priesthood has consequences. One is *either* "responsible for the rubrics" *or* "responsive to the spirit of Vatican II." There were no two ways about it, for a while. It became divisive, this new developing vision of priesthood in the face of the call to discipleship.

In the moment of my ordination our beloved Church was still basking in the afterglow of Vatican II. I was sent to Arizona to work in a parish for a year; the training at that time included, as a requirement of our theological course of study, after six months of non-permanent diaconate working in a church, the newly ordained priest working in the parochial apostolate for another year. My experience at St. Pius X in Tucson was blessed in so many ways. The people felt empowered. They had an active parish council and many people working in social justice, as well as a deeply involved congregation well informed about the ritual worship cycle. A case in point on the social justice front was a program which interfaced the culture of West Tucson with that of East Tucson—the people on the west side of town tended more toward poverty and tribal or Mexican ethnic lifestyles. The ones on the east, "at Pius," were wealthier but alien, immigrants, as it were, to the southwest from other parts of the US. (I was initially amazed at how many parishioners were "from back East" meaning Albuquerque or Galveston!) So there was a sharing of funds in a sense but it was not degrading to the people who embodied the rich indigenous cultures of Indian civilizations and Central American migrants, and the descendants of the ancient displaced former Mexican imperial or republican hegemonies. The parish was so Vatican II, and the people felt no compunction about telling the priests, especially perhaps the younger ones, how to become the new kind of priest that seemed *required* by the ecclesiology implied by *The Church in the Modern World*. I remember fondly how Grace Bousek, a well educated woman with theological training, told me that I had really blundered by announcing, "the second reading from St. Paul's Letter to the Hebrews," which Grace pointed out, strongly but kindly, was well known to have been scripted by a different hand, a different theology, and consequently most definitely not Paul's letter at all. Chastened, I learned. The involvement of the people with the liturgy was intelligent, inquisitive, reverent, respectful, and creative. I learned a great deal about how and where the Spirit blows.

There were also people who were quite unenthusiastic about the changes in the Liturgy. They were mostly military retirees, to be honest, brought up in the era before not only the Second Vatican Council but before the Second World War. Their Church was strong and ancient, unchanging across the globe and unchanging in time. They were devastated by the turning of the altar, the personality of the priests now so evident, and the need to examine practices, even questioning the place of the rosary during the consecration, or the possibility of receiving Eucharist at the hands of laywomen. The things that bothered them so much seemed of such little consequence to me at the time. With more time and experience I have learned a great deal about how we all must listen to one another and be more patient—like Job, like God. Because the Spirit blows where She will.

I believe that I was then a "young man seeing visions." I have become an "old man dreaming dreams." The clarity of my relationship with the Lord Jesus was so strong, and had been so solidly "felt" for so many years before and after my ordination. I was strongly aware of the changes in the Church as being the work of my Friend and I could see His hand in so much of my own trying to love as He does, and to pray with the people in His name, that I just couldn't comprehend people being so worried about how the world as they knew it was being displaced, replaced by new open-ended discussions about the meaning of everything in the Church. They felt as though things told to us by the Mother of God were true and were yet being disregarded, that things which were of the apostolic Tradition were being lost, that the whole "economy of salvation" was, now, deposited in a Church becoming bankrupt. I had little time or understanding. But I am learning.

My next career move, as some might see it, was to become a college professor. I moved to a Jesuit university, which was looking to widen its offerings in the Arts, as a response to a recognized fault in the liberal arts training that its students were receiving. My academic training as well as my personal dedication to painting as a way to self-knowledge, and honestly, as another call from God, made me seem the perfect fit for this place. My liturgical experience here burgeoned into a kind of personal apostolate. It was rather wonderful for me to be part of something to which I could contribute, but which seemed to be under the control or the guidance of something, someone Other than me.

My work was to be part of a team building an art department from scratch almost. But I considered that an extension of my call to be a priest in everything, to find God in all things, to play the hand I'm dealt. I found that my practice of priesthood was intimately involved in the building of community within the defining walls of this particular place in academe.

A kind of personal apostolate, steeped in my field in the classroom and, yet, made manifest in rituals for a larger community within this particular academic world, caused innumerable problems, as one might imagine. The need for masses which spoke in Vatican II language was quite apparent in the faces of students who came to my dormitory living room every Sunday night. We sat on the floor, shared the homily, prayed for family, friends, church, and world events, well into the night. I became quite adept at finding, with God's help, recorded music, from many sources, which would help the readings to penetrate the souls or minds of the small congregation. So we listened to rock, jazz, classical, romantic, Gregorian, Palestrina, Gabrielli, Fauré, Rachmaninoff, Kachaturian, Gershwin, the Beatles, Radiohead, and Depeche Mode. The music really helped the readings seem more immediately relevant to the experience of my young friends around the altar.

I moved on to graduate studies in New York, Boston, and Venice, working on a doctorate at NYU, which eventuated in a much greater understanding of my craft and calling as a painter. Studies in the history of church interior architecture, environments for liturgy, led me to a dissertation about the evolving multiple meanings in liturgical practice and the infrastructures built up over the millennia of ritual evolution. The dissertation was entitled *Sacred Space: An Aesthetic for the Liturgical Environment* (published in 1985 by Wyndham Hall Press). It looked at the evolution of both the liturgy from apostolic times and the places which were developed to house the rituals of the people of God.

When I returned to university life, my hunger for doing good liturgy was greatly enhanced by the desire of the students for a late night Mass on Sunday nights. Combined with the reluctance of the local sacerdotal community to preside at a late hour, my involvement developed into a singular apostolate for well over a decade. The mass grew in popularity and in length; praying seemed comfortable and intense in the student body. These students stayed every week for well over an hour, praying, listening to music, sitting in silence late into the night, visiting before and after. It was a good thing. It was for many of us a "base community," an embodiment of all I'd been trained to encourage in the post Vatican II Church.

There were other opinions, however. Some thought that, if the mass were popular, I must be doing something illicit to make the students like me——rather than to seek the Lord in their midst, I suppose. Some thought that if the previous assumption were true, that the archdiocese would be sending spies to report on the irregularities. I was told by a couple of officials of the local Jesuit Community and from the Campus Ministry staff, that if such visitation would indeed happen, and if the visitors should find problems, which they'd report, and, if the Cardinal should send a warning, then "we will not defend you." I was on my own.

There were complaints from some conservative students, but other students took care of that quite handily. Their mass wasn't going to be taken from them. They wrote in the student newspaper or argued face to face. Then, when a number of other priests found that they could afford to preside late at night, the burden of presiding every Sunday night of the school year for more than a decade, became a shared responsibility. I kept doing the music for that late night community for a couple of years, until the university music minister found reason to consider recorded music immoral, especially if any pieces were not written specifically for sacred use. The backlash seems to have come from the liturgical musician in my case. To be honest, he was not alone in the Church in this opinion. Opposition grew. The things we were doing, like long prayers of the faithful, long silent periods, lots of tears and feelings of being a community who would welcome anybody, became points of disagreement. Eventually, I was forced out of the stable. I no longer preside often on campus. It is painful, but there are crowds who attend liturgy, who do service. The presiders are my brothers, they are well prepared, preach well, and are not considered embarrassing. My own feelings of being *anathema*-come-lately cause me constant grief when I do attend functions in the chapel, but they are also an invitation from God to be more humble. I remember the "conversation" between the Lord of her mystical encounters and Catherine of Siena. The Lord said, "I am, you are not."

On the deepest level of my calling from the Lord and the Church, I am content to be *nothing* in this spiritual sense. I am like Siddhartha, before becoming the Buddha, depending on being "awake" to the enlightenment which abides in nothingness. On the other hand, I find a great learning about the meaning of priesthood, which might be a help to the rest of the Church at this time when we are soon to contemplate another ecumenical council to move deeper into the new millennium.

Over the years I have come to see that there are two ways of being called to the Church as priest, and I see that they are at least contrary in their outlook on just what a priest does, whom he serves, where, and how he finds his role in the Church. The two contraries have biblical traditions going back to the very foundation of Israel; longer ago than Jesus, the roles of priests were defined. The Lord, the good and gracious Godly Jew, took His liturgical training from the Scriptures. I see now that there are two ways of being priest even in His own understanding, as imparted by his immediate disciples.

The contraries have to be addressed with the swinging of the pendulum, differing approaches to service in the living mechanism, which is Christ's Body, the Church. The book which follows is an attempt to understand the polar pulling, in so many situations, on the mind and heart of the priest. He is often torn between adherence and attentiveness, between following rules and following the Spirit, between keeping the Church consistent and keeping her open. The pendulum swings in the very clockwork of every priest's apostolate. The trick is to keep it swinging so that the clock continues to tell the tenor of the times—as Jesus would have us do in His own reading of the priestly reality of His Jerusalem Temple.

There is great pain when priests can only see one way of being priest. We must be awake to the Holy Spirit wherever *It* blows. We must be aware constantly that the little "still, small voice," calls us to truth and faithful commitment to *It*, to trust and hopeful openness to the others sent by *It*, to love and a free following of the One High Priest, emptying the self for the sake of the kingdom according to His relationship to the Father and to *It*. Attentiveness to the Holy Spirit, adherence to *Its* rules, is paramount.

2

Introit

I will go up to the altar of God, to God who gives joy to my youth.

Self-observation Promotes
a *Cause Célèbre in Pectore*

A joyful beginning

I've been a priest for thirty-five years, a Jesuit for forty-five. My education since the beginning of my professional life has been steeped in the rhetoric and ideology of Vatican II. My training was quite open-ended. I was always encouraged to think and to pray, to seek relationship with the Lord, according to the dicta of both the Society of Jesus and Mother Church. The whole enterprise was like therapy for so long, helping me to overcome a pre-Vatican II education bathed in guilt and self-abnegation. For me it was a liberation from not so much my own family's *praxis* but from what seemed a centuries' old way of being Catholic. We knew we were different.

Consequently, the priesthood which I'd found myself practicing, one which I enjoyed and which encouraged others to think, to pray, and to act according to conscience, was also a liberation. I guess I'm a post-Vatican II priest. Many think of me as liberal, but the ensuing pages will probably show a deeply conservative motivation under that surface. In the early 'eighties while I was working on the dissertation as part of my training as a painter at NYU, I'd found that my need for a terminal degree in Art was compromised by my job at a Catholic (formerly men's only) college. The particular academic environment at St. Joseph's implied that art (and the terminal MFA) would not be politically suitable for a Jesuit in academic life here. When the opportunity came to get a Ph.D., it seemed only natural to compromise and to pursue credentials, which would make me "one of the boys." I would have a chance, I thought, of becoming the first full-time tenured faculty member in the Arts at this place. Sad to say, it would be a coup.

The degree led to a couple of lectures given to prestigious audiences, to architecture students at the University of Pennsylvania, for instance, or to theological professionals at the Catholic Theological Society of America, and to liturgists, architects, and liturgical environmentalists at the Form/Reform conference in San Diego. The degree, combined with a need to explain what I'd learned in my studies about art and church, coalesced in this dialogue within a committed and deep-thinking community. My painting and my *priesting* were working together with my teaching to make a creditable academic and apostolic life. I found my vocation to be blessed in that many friends and acquaintances were sharing a belief and a devotion to the possibility of God. I liked my life.

I wrote some books, too. The essence of my four decades' study is a stance which celebrates a view of Church—inclusive, supportive, open to new ways of considering ages-old revelations. In short, I found myself becoming freer still, and my priesthood was helping others to find freedom in the Lord.

The big however

In the period since the end of Vatican II, however, I have had the necessity of learning to protect myself from the guilt of being freer.

I have come to see myself in others' eyes as a liberal. This doesn't mean simply that I am in favor of taking care of the poor, the widow, and the orphan; apparently it means that I am a libertine, one who would drop everything true and holy in order to promulgate my liberal agenda—the liberal agenda coming from being in art and doing liturgy with more theatrical drama than the norm. Train an artist; get an artist. But do we want an artist? That's an important question.

The evidentiary examples which I relate were profoundly provocative experiences for me, successes in ministry, countered too often by cruelty from bureaucracy. I needed to be kept at bay for my *excesses*. This sounds ridiculous, of course, and self-absorbed. But years after feeling thus victimized, and after years of prayer, I come to grips with my frustration, in dialogue with confessors, friends, scholars, therapists, and the Lord Himself, and I find forgiveness for my detractors. However, in the words of John F. Kennedy, when asked how he, a Catholic and a politician, could abide by the dictum to "forgive thine enemies," said, "I always forgive my enemies; I just never forget their names." An important distinction, because it says that we can love those who hurt us while not denying the effect of choices and actions which cause undue pain and the unjust *retention* of the wages of sin. I take the word from the somewhat murky translation in the gospels of the right of the Church to "retain sins"— *Whose sins you forgive; they are forgiven them. Whose sins you retain; they are retained*—Forgiveness is paramount to living a Christlike life. But…

Who's coming to church?

The cruelty of bureaucracy shows in a response to the company I keep. When I first lived in a dormitory, as recounted above, I would say Mass in my room, and some of my residents would join me. It was *de rigeur* in those days that religious would say Mass in a "private oratory" rather than in a church. Congregants were preferred. So this was liturgy according to the tradition and according to the newer inclusive and less formal approach that I'd learned in theological training. The mass became popular with students, eventually becoming too large for my living room; it became campus-wide, a regular offering of the Campus Ministry program.

In point of fact, many times over the ten years or so, there were suspicious dark-suited, FBI types who came to mass and who seemed to be observing in the name of the Holy Office—but at the end of mass they would invariably seek me out, shake my hand, and thank me for a beautiful mass. It was long but apparently it was rubrically correct.

The music minister told me that many students said that they liked the liturgy to my face, but that they told him that they were only "being nice" so as not to hurt me; they really hated what I did. He was also heard to tell his compatriots on the Campus Ministry Team, "Dennis does bring lots of people back to the Church—but they're the wrong people—and we don't want them." I think something else might have been at stake for him than that I was doing liturgy in a way that he didn't like, but that's something between him and God.

Other complaints included a kind of denigration of the whole Vatican II initiative. I found an implied preferred *retrogradation* in this comment from a superior who also had power on campus: "You say the post-Vatican II liturgy better than anyone else in the Delaware Valley; this must stop!" The explanation was even more confounding: "Nobody else can do what you're doing. The kids like this and they'll never have the opportunity to experience it again after they leave here. You are doing them a tremendous disservice by giving them a taste for liturgy which will never be satisfied in a parish."

This is undoubtedly my own cross to bear. I have learned after the opportunity for doing such liturgy was removed—politically rather than by any overt confrontation—that I am offered by the Lord an insight into the very experience of Being, an offer to join in God's own learning to love us anyway. Remember how YHWH was continually disappointed in the Old Testament, always asking prophets like *Isaiah 1-3*, or *Jeremiah, Ezekiel, Micah, Hosea*, and the ever-reluctant *Jonah* to tell the people how hurt and angry He was at their dropping Him in favor of idols for their own gratification? I find, after much heart-rending supplication, that God offers for those who love Him (as Paul says in *Romans* 8:28) to make good come from anything. I choose to love Him and to let this go. It's hard sometimes to realize that my liturgical ministry has been rejected; but I am invited to suffer with Jesus: sympathize, empathize, to become compassionate, in other words. Life's lessons, as says Aeschylus in *The Agamemnon* come from suffering. No pain, no gain!

Instruction comes in examining structures

There are wider lessons to learn. One of them includes this: the rejection of the liturgical motivations envisioned and invited by the documents of Vatican II is a wide-spread consequence of the present desire for structure, order, centralization, and control, prevalent not only in the Roman Church but evident, too, in so many other religious and political institutions around the globe.

I am wondering, naturally, if my experience is in any way normal or normative. Do other priests have this difficulty of being seen as a threat? Are they, without much in the way of due process, then "necessarily" put into a position wherein they are not allowed to perform or to preside because they are unconventional or considered too difficult to mimic?

My scholarly pursuits have been deeply enmeshed in the creation and experience of environments for the human encounter with the numinous God, in the community, in nature, in the dark, within the self. In working through *Sacred Space: An Aesthetic for the Liturgical Environment*, we discovered that there are things that make the numinous experience of mystery, or encounter with the *kratophanic, hierophanic, or theophanic* self-manifestation of the Other, easier to recognize. Those things are environmental. Darkness, silence, emptiness, monumentality, profusion, and progressive entry into the holiest of places are all atmospheric helps to the awareness of the numinous. Focus is an elemental necessity, but atmosphere can encourage focus.

The history of sacred places indicates that focus is maintained in either a long or a round plan, with the attention directed either forward or centrally. I was instrumental, because of my scholarly pursuits, in the arrangement of two of our campus holy spaces, two liturgical places, one for the Jesuit community and the other for the entire university community. Due to my own training and my own preconceptions, I felt that the direction of liturgical development in the twentieth century, especially after the Vatican Council, was toward the circular, the centrally-focused space. It seemed that the emphasis on the *people of God* and the concurrent awareness of the *priesthood of the people* were coalescing in such a way as to make the Eucharistic experience more central, among the people rather than in front of them. The longitudinally focused tradition, with all the action up front, in vogue since the Council of Trent, was to be changed after Vatican II by a liturgical and Eucharistic awareness of Christ among us.

The vertical approach to God, as evidenced in the high-peaked ogival arcades of French Gothic architecture, and the longitudinal approach, as exemplified in the long horizontal cornices of English Perpendicular, had become a norm after the sixteenth century Council and the consequent Missal of Pius V. The motivation of the Second Vatican Council was clearly, whether horizontal or vertical, to focus both the community of the faithful and the sacerdotal community centrally on the Eucharist. The difference in the two *foci*, of course, is that the Eucharist is central but in the round plan always seen against a backdrop of the People of God. The old privileged, hierarchical place of the cult leader would necessarily be compromised. The priest in the middle of the people is quite different from the priest elevated at the end of the nave.

The fact is that many church architects and designers struggled for the latter half of the twentieth century with how to *center* the congregation on the Eucharist, while paying attention to a newfound concentration on the biblical Tradition and the need to *evangelize* through the homiletic prerogative and duty of the ordained. Many east-facing congregations found their churches refocused at the crossing. Gothic and Romanesque churches were easily configured with the sanctuary in front of the choir instead of behind it. The change came gradually and not without reluctance, but it did come. The "newer" arrangements were much more like the ages-old arrangement at St. Peter's Basilica. The plan and section of the big urban cathedral churches, by the end of the century, had, for the most part, conformed to this new centralization of the Eucharist. The seats of the congregation were put into a cruciform "centripetalization," as it were, with nave, two transepts, and choir focused on the space in the crossing, under the dome or the central lantern.

My two local examples

THE UNIVERSITY CHAPEL

The two chapels that I'd had some hand in designing here on campus, were, like all those other post Vatican II places, focused on the center. The main campus chapel, which easily holds 500 congregants, had a raised sanctuary platform with altar, ambo, and presidential seat, placed squarely under the crossing of the quadripartite, groined vault, under an evanescent cruciform skylight.

After ten years of these arrangements, the new chapel (1992) was rearranged so that the moveable sanctuary furniture was replaced with much heavier and unmovable altar and ambo. The whole sanctuary was also shifted north so that the choir was actually pushed to the side and the sanctuary came much closer to the organ in the north of the chapel space. The central focus was almost completely re-oriented (and not toward the east but toward the north). Other changes in the plan of the whole chapel complex included removing the chapel of repose which had been a small sky-lighted chapel to the west of the gathering space, with a glazed, fenestrated wall by which the gathering congregation could attend to the presence of the Eucharist in the tabernacle, either by looking through a floor to ceiling vertical opening or through a horizontal window with a shelf which served as ambry, housing the oil of chrism, oil of catechumens, and oil of the sick. This arrangement of the ambry and tabernacle was balanced on the other side of the gathering space by the baptismal pool and font, which in our chapel, looks sarcophageal; so, where the paschal candle resides, the font itself images death into life. This allowed for the people, while passing into the sacred space for liturgy, to literally pass through the sacrament and sacramentals of entrance and exit, the *viaticum,* the ambry of sacred oils, the baptistry, and the paschal candle, reminding any aware member of the community that they pass through life, beginning to end, entering with Jesus into His death so that they might rise with Him into eternal life. The people would be reminded of the community's rites of passage on the way to Eucharist. Indeed, the baptismal font is arranged so that any adult being immersed after RCIA would be facing away from the main sanctuary entering down into the pool and would rise out of it to face the altar after receiving the initiating sacrament. The whole entrance and exit of the chapel should be a meditative experience, separating the sacred from the profane space.

But with the renovation after the first decade, it was decided that the Eucharist needed to be present in the daily chapel during the daily mass. The oils needed no proximity to the viaticum within the tabernacle nor to the baptistry. The passage between the birth/death/resurrection accoutrements was lost with the new arrangement. The old chapel of repose, which would allow three or four to rest with the tabernacle, now became a sky-lit and large windowed counseling chamber for confessions and counsel.

A lot was lost, but it is now much more comfortable as a mid-twentieth-century chapel, with the priest and the pulpit in the "front where they belong."The presider no longer has the inconvenience of having to address two different sides of the chapel when preaching. It is just like class, and the preacher need never move from the comfort of the lectern.

THE JESUIT COMMUNITY CHAPEL

The Jesuit house chapel had the altar at one end, the ambo at the entrance so that the community could reverence the Book as well as the altar when entering either as a community for prayer or as individuals coming to meditate. The tabernacle was behind the altar and the presidential seat to one side. The other seats for the sacerdotal community were arranged antiphonally, forty-five *in toto*.

The rearrangement of this space, after ten years of this darkly silent, monumental and antiphonal set up, included re-covering all the upholstered seats. Now they are mauve instead of the 1990s dark blue (which had comfortably made reference to the dominant cobalt of the simple stained glass, inherited from the chapel's 1959 original construction). It also included replacing the six-year-old blue carpet with a light beige one. The pecan paneled walls were painted a similar light beige. This all seemed like a simple change in taste, wasteful in some sense because the blue and brown were hardly worn. But the real change came in putting the altar and ambo side by side at the "front where they belong" and rearranging the antiphonal seating of the sacerdotal community into five rows on each side of a central aisle so that the congregation again faces the priest who can preach without having to turn from left to right.

A reflection on the implications of furniture for infrastructure

The rearrangement of furniture bothered me extremely. Others seem relatively unperturbed. I was particularly nonplussed by both decorating *agents* taking pains to keep me (and most others from both communities) out of the loop while decisions were being made to change what we had done. My deeper difficulty, however, finds its source in the realization that the two reconfigurations imply, within my very own academic and religious community, a decision to go back to a time when the priest was in charge of the church, when the people were not co-operators in the priesthood of Christ but observant correspondents who cooperate with the priesthood of the clergy by paying attention to what they say and showing support in the collection. It is somehow sadly about power.

On another front and in another place in *Fearsome Edifice: a History of the Decorated DOMUS in Catholic Churches* (Wyndham Hall 2003), my second book, we have looked at how the liturgical space has been a virtual grandfather's clock with a pendulum swinging constantly during the Church's development. The decoration in all styles and periods, Byzantine, Romanesque, Gothic, Renaissance, Baroque, Rococo, etc., has been championed by those in favor of *la luxe* for the Lord, on the one hand, and those favoring austerity for God's people, on the other. The present time likewise has proponents for each, the conflation of historical dialogue being aided by instant global communication.

The trouble with the move from round to long plans in liturgical spaces is, as I see it, indicative of a larger political reality. The worldwide choice of order over chaos has recently taken on the appearance of a universal choice in favor of obedience to authority. The Church in these troubled times seems intent on making sure that the clergy are at the center of things, (so that, perhaps, we'll not be able to get into trouble?).

The move is strange just now, given the strength of the Church's drive to democratize in the middle of the last century. It is also painful in light of the recent most public debacle over child-abuse and diocesan cover-ups. The bishops (Greek: *hoi epi-skopoi*, overseers) have morphed into overlords. The moral leadership of the bishops has been greatly impinged upon by the press making bishops look like recalcitrant CEO's who are ambitious and unwilling to take risks. The bishops are, of course, getting a bum rap, perhaps. But the impression remains that they are not exactly trustworthy.

Against this backdrop, to have the more conservative leadership continually push for less inclusive dominance over the prayer life of the faithful and an implied exclusive control over the political choices which are to be made by the faithful, is a *skandalion*, a little pebble constantly making walking difficult. The pebble, the scandal of leadership in the Church, should be embraced as a penance, I suppose, but it should not be imposed by that very leadership. This is, as I see it, a burdensome difficulty in the Church today.

Implications for priests

The rest of this book is written to suggest that we need to re-examine the very basis of leadership in the Church of Jesus, who said, in fact, "Call no man father for you have one Father in heaven....and call no one teacher for there is one teacher and Lord." (*Matthew* 23) What does it mean to be a priest? How can one claim a *vocation*?

The book takes a look at how this one priest has tried to reconcile his relationship with God and his religious community with his role as cult shaman among the Catholic faithful—socially, historically, ecclesiastically, theologically, and ethically—a role built upon millennia of development, while still based in that essential relationship to the Mystery, a relationship with the Lord, Christ. In short, the priest of Aaron is actually ordained a priest of Melchizedek and must make sense of it.

My hope is that this reflection will help others to think through the role of priesthood in their lives, whether they are practitioners, clients, or distant observers.

3

Gradual

Let us go up to the altar of God, step by step

The truth about good liturgical practice—what could it possibly become at this point in history? For many the questions have all been recently answered with the *General Instruction on the Roman Missal* (GIRM). There are very strong recommendations and some straightforward rules on what to do, what not to do, and how to think about the present movements in liturgical practice. We are awaiting the response to a new set of rules for the English speaking world—that promises to be interesting!

For others the questions about good liturgical practice cannot be reduced to rules. I am afraid that I sit in that camp. There is for me a call from the Lord, as well as from the People of God, to use all that I know, all that I am, (heart, mind, soul, and strength) to help the people pray whenever I preside at any liturgical function. This is what we were taught in the heady days of theological training after the last Vatican Council had issued its documents on the meaning of the Church, liturgical prayer, the question of membership, the role of the laity, etc.

In *Sacred Space: An Aesthetic for the Liturgical Environment*, we looked at the development of liturgical spaces from the beginning of the history of the Church, just after the death, resurrection, and ascension of the Lord. Our belief has been that the Holy Spirit, ever since Pentecost, has been with the Church of Jesus and has breathed God's own life, the communal life and love of the Trinity, into our prayer. The history of liturgical practice is, however, fraught with pendulum swings from the more structured to the more spirited. Germain Bazin implies that all art history will indicate a constantly swinging pendulum in the transition of artistic practice from the balance and symmetry of the *classical* to the asymmetry and romance of the *baroque*. This image is useful for us in the consideration of liturgical history and the present watershed of liturgical practice.

In *Fearsome Edifice: A History of the Decorated Domus in Catholic Churches*, we looked at the way in which conflict over the very meaning of liturgy has changed the practice continually in the history of the Church. *Semper reformanda*, continually **needing** to reform or change (an implication of the gerundive in Latin), the Church has given us a rich history of symbol, music, drama, dress, and reverence in the environs of our Sacred Liturgy. Of particular interest, in one of the chapters of that book (Chapter nine, "Fine Finish for Furnishings") we examine the paradigmatic shift of practices epitomized in the changing of the shape and function of the altar.

...to God, the joy of our youth

The Hebrew history of communal prayer included a large altar on which priests could climb and sacrifice animals. There were large corners, which were called "the horns of the altar." The Ark of the Covenant carrying the sacred scriptures, the Decalogue along with other writings, resided within the Holy of Holies; the sacrifices took place with more public accessibility. The *bema* was a platform from which the Torah could be read or preached about. There are some obvious correlations between Temple worship and the development of ritual spaces for Christians within the Empire. For instance, the Romans had an *exedra,* a raised platform against an apsidal wall in many basilicas, for the reading of the laws of the Republic or the will of the emperor. However, another tradition of ritual sacrifice, without animals, took place in the Dionysiac rites of the ancient Greeks, developing into the theatres of the Periclean Age, with their platform altars, *skene* walls with doors and upper windows (the quintessential back wall of the Baroque sanctuary), and proscenium for the ritual, dramatically enacted in tragedies and comedies, with lots of blood spoken of but never shed on stage. The image also lent itself to the ritual practices and mere dramatic presentations of Roman theatre and pretty soon to liturgical settings for the early Christians.

The altar took on, according to Josef Jungmann (*Missarum Solemnia,* volumes one and two), many different symbolic forms. In the earliest scenarios for the Eucharist, there were no permanent facilities; the presider sat or stood at a temporary table on which the ritual meal, the *agape* of the Passover, of the Last Supper, of the Crucified and Resurrected Lord, was commemorated. The table was primarily something on which to place the bread and wine.

Since the liturgy developed so closely with the understanding of Resurrection, there was a marked connection between the "Church suffering, militant, and triumphant." The relationship of the Eucharist to the connection of the living with the dead was particularly pronounced when celebrated in cemeteries or catacombs, but it became common to commemorate the dead by including some relic of their earthly life at, under, or on the altar. This soon devolved into a dedicated altar, which looked more solid and had enclosed relics under or within the *mensa* itself. The altar began to look more like a sarcophagus. It must have seemed a natural shift from table to stone box (and eventually to solid stone with small relics incorporated in the altar stone).

In the ninth century, the Carolingian court began to incorporate a kind of worship of the eucharistic presence, replete with monstrance, to accommodate the unleavened disc which the court had developed for just such reverence. Here the west begins a long experience of the host, the disk of bread. The monstrance soon grew to include the entire altar, the monstrance becoming visually framed by *reredos*, *retable*, and, analogically, in the Eastern Churches, *ikonostases*. The table had become a stone, imaging the blessed dead, including the Lord, the *reredos* most often displaying the Risen Christ, the Crucified (in a "Rood Screen"), the Ascension, or some other moment in Christ's life which would be ritually "re-presented." In Dom Odo Casel's memorable description of how the transubstantiation is effected, Jesus is present again, by God's power, through the priest's words and action; the Lord transcends time and space and enters into our time and space. He is a virtual "time lord." According to Mircea Eliade's immortal coining of the Latin phrase into the vernacular, *in illo tempore*, "at that time" or, prosaically, "once upon a time," God did something with mankind, through an act with a human. At Mass, God re-enters our dimensional existence and Jesus lives again with us, present, real, soul and body, humanity and divinity. These descriptions are essential truths in the Catholic churches; they become dogma and not merely poetic opinions but unassailable revelation. The accoutrements of the altar took on the responsibility of proclaiming these mind-boggling realities.

More recently, with the liturgical renewal leading up to Vatican Council II and proclaimed in the documents thereof, there has evolved the *coram populo* altar, the table within the body of the congregation, recapturing the earliest images of the altar just after the Lord initiated the practice of Eucharist on that table in the Upper Room of the Last Supper.

The altar which had become relatively removed—from table, to tomb, to throne, to backdrop for the mysterious and mystical maneuvers of the priest, who had learned to pray facing east, according to the prescription for right ritual ensconced in the Missal of Pius V following the liturgical renewal which preceded and followed the sixteenth century Council of Trent, with the tremendous influences, since referred to as the Reformation, the Counter-Reformation and the Enlightenment—the altar became again a table in the midst of the assembly.

In the ninth chapter of *Fearsome Edifice* we learned that there is a new renewal growing in the Church, evidenced in the development of a new Post-Vatican II "restoration" of the liturgy, exemplified in the design of the altar. In that chapter we learn of the exchanging of the large refectory table altar in the center of the crossing of Notre Dame de Paris for a solid bronze-faced box on a raised platform in the same center of the great cathedral. The box has sculpture on its faces. There doesn't seem to be anything within but the box looks like a reliquary or a jewelry box, something which holds hidden treasure. It has something of the quality of a portable safe. The paradigm has shifted again, from table to treasury.

Archbishop Rembert Weakland OSB records (*Commonweal,* January 2002) the change of the name of the "sanctuary" in recent Roman documents, to the "*presbyterium.*" He argues that this is significant of something counter to the spirit of the Vatican Council II. There is food for thought in considering how little changes in words and symbols both articulate changes and encourage them. The possibility that Weakland is right finds evidence in the threatening strength of the "reformists" who attend liturgy with notebooks, so that they might record and report "aberrations" from the norms required by the newly politically correct watchdogs who would remove anything that smacks of innovation, free thinking, tender emotion, or a dreaded *intimacy* of any kind in the expression of the prayer of the Church, which might offend the most reserved of the faithful. Everything must be formal or it is wrong for them. "Presbyterium" has become standard.

I believe, from my own experience, that the dread of intimacy can lead to incredibly hard-line responses from the powerful to the felt needs of the stricken. The Pharisee who thanked God that he was not like the wretched publican who humbly stood in the back of the synagogue is for me an image of the righteous who cannot entertain informality in Church. It scares them. I am afraid that if all informality is removed from the liturgy, that the Church will again be in need of a reform, a great endeavor on the part of the Holy Spirit to get us back on track. She, Wisdom Herself, is elusive, not predictable; gentle, not enslaving; intimate, not bombastic. How can we pretend to be people whose Advocate is the Paraclete, and not allow for "the wind to blow where It will"?

4

First Reading

A reading from the book of personal experience

There was a time when I was very proud to be asked by students or family members to preside at weddings, baptisms, and funerals. I felt very much the chosen priest, like I was appreciated not only for the way I said Mass but for who I was. It was a humbling thought, but a very comfortable one. This seems to be a common experience for the newly ordained. I found that I wanted to do the very best for the people who cared enough to ask me to take part in these most significant moments of their lives. I must admit I was asked more than the Jesuit norm for one whose life is spent in academe. For a while I was affiliated with an Arizona parish as an associate pastor, but to be honest it was for only a year and some months in my whole thirty-five years as a priest, in my whole forty-five as a Jesuit. I have presided at hundreds of liturgies celebrating life's passages, nonetheless.

I have discovered that there might have been other, less than personally flattering, reasons for choosing a visiting priest to preside at these important events. Sometimes I was not so much the priest of choice as any priest other than the one in the parish! The reflections of this essay are the consequence of some necessary conclusions about some priestly encounters that friends might have had in the normal course of their parochial experience. The stories that I am going to tell right now will remind the reader, I'm sure, of similar episodes in her/his own memory, which have caused interior questions about the very nature of priesthood. Here are three stories: about a wedding, a baptism, and a funeral:

The wedding

The couple were friends from school. He had been a real help in my department at the university; he'd been a most industrious and kind work-study student. "Work-studies" help to pay their tuition by taking on jack-of-all-trades service jobs on campus. He and I had become friends; I always knew I could depend on him to get last-minute glasses or cheese for a gallery reception, or to help hang the student show, or to order materials for class. He was a great kid and I was very proud and happy to be asked to help with his marriage ceremony. We talked innumerable times, he and his bride and I. We became closer. By the time of the wedding, I knew her pretty well, too.

The pastor said that they could have an "outside priest" do the Mass but not to expect himself to be anywhere around because he was much too busy. On the day of the rehearsal, one of the curates came to open the church for us and told us we were most welcome and that we could do whatever seemed good to us. He just asked that I make sure that everything be put back where it belonged. I felt quite comfortable.

As had become my custom, we took a long time with the rehearsal, starting with prayer, going through the motions of the ritual, making sure that everybody knew why we were doing the candle lighting this way, what praying at Mary's altar would mean, what a sacrament is, how important it is to pray for your friends on their wedding day during the reflection period before the Post Communion, and the like. I want most of all that the couple will spend a few precious seconds, side-by-side, aware of the Lord. I figure I can get a little bit under the skin of the friends and family of the couple, take them seriously and encourage their best understanding of what the Church is and how it works in this very particular instance. It took two hours this time. I didn't mind, really, because universally everyone involved, each time I do this, seems to be growing in awareness of the sacramental nature of marriage; it feels as if this growth will color the whole future for this couple and their "community."

At any rate, on the next day, the day of the wedding, the pastor came to the church. He became quite concerned because we were using pink candles and the mothers were prepared to light them for the ceremony at the very beginning. It seems that his reading of the "universal law of the Church" demands that we use white candles exclusively. Because we had rehearsed it this way, however, with the permission of his curate, he allowed this to go on. But his own discomfort made me feel quite guilty, even though I knew he was not quite right on the question of the law at that time.

At the end of the Mass, which went beautifully and smoothly, the pastor let me know his wrath because the couple had lit the paschal candle, thinking it a more fit symbol of the presence of the Lord in their sacrament than the store-bought wedding candle, which could have no ecclesial function other than that it would sit on their dining room table until dust or waste had seen its demise. This is a beautiful "read" on the uniting of Baptism vows with Wedding vows, and the expressed hope that this marriage would make a place for the Lord in the lives of everyone their marriage touched, until their deaths. Two candles were lit by their mothers, representing their own baptisms, and the one paschal candle indicating that in this sacramental union their separate lives could light the fire of Christ. This is good theological reflection, I thought. The pastor in retrospect thought otherwise.

46 ▶   The Priest and the Pendulum

He thought so much otherwise, in fact, that he told the parents immediately after the wedding was over that he doubted its validity. He came back into his church to reprimand me for having done another unthinkable thing—I had allowed members of the laity to sit unconscionably close to the tabernacle. He was quite agitated. This all happened, as I remember, ten years after the Vatican Council documents on liturgy and twenty years before the retrogressive GIRM (*General Instruction on the Roman Missal*).

There was no reconciling in sight. I had promised the curate that I would get everything back in its place. I was doing that when the pastor came back to the sanctuary. After the tirade to the families, in a completely different voice and mode, he said that I shouldn't bother with putting things away; he was perfectly happy to do that as a good host. With that he proceeded to pick up the still warm paschal candle. Though it seemed like poetic justice, or even a holy reprimand from God at the time, I did not say anything untoward when he poured hot wax onto his own head. I was glad, in fact, that he hadn't done any real damage to himself. But I still feel quite guilty at the strength of his discomfort. So, that's the wedding story. The couple is still married and parenting well, two decades later.

The Baptism

This couple asked me to fly to the "tri-state area" to baptize their second child. I had known them for a year when they were first pregnant after a very long time married and hoping for children. Just before I'd left Arizona they discovered that they were about to become parents. The months had been full of excitement and gratitude, but then something went horribly wrong. The baby was lost and his mother was deeply depressed, gaining weight and unable to shake the blues. Months later the doctors were amazed to discover that she was still pregnant with the twin of the boy who had died. This twin became an amazing young man. He helped my friends to move to North Carolina. Eventually they had a little girl from God's great love. They asked me to baptize her with them in the only Catholic parish in a strongly southern, tri-state, "fringe" area in the Bible Belt.

I flew south to baptize the baby for this blessed couple. I was so happy for them and so aware of how faithful they were, how full of gratitude to God. I feel as though this couple displays the essence of what we mean when we speak of the "leadership of the laity." These two had been through such personal disappointment. Fear of losing another child had been, almost, but not quite, crippling. These are good people with great love, good education, good jobs, and a tremendous generosity. They believed, like the Virgin Mother in the Lucan narrative of the Visitation, that God would be true to His promise.

The pastor said that they could have a "visiting priest" do the baptism, but only if he would agree to preside at Sunday liturgy and preach, because he himself was much too busy to do it. I agreed. That all seemed fine and reasonable to me. When I got to the church and met the music ministers, the eucharistic ministers, the readers, and acolytes, I was deeply moved by how intelligent they all seemed and how gracious to me, the stranger, to this "silicon valley of the east."

Then the pastor, not quite "too busy," came into the sacristy. They all became very quiet. He did not say hello but told me to get dressed. I asked where the vestments were. Annoyed, he showed me the right closet door. As I was getting robed, he reminded me that I had to preach, because he was too busy. He said, "keep it short." I was a little nonplussed, having worked especially hard on the homily because I was among strangers and my "performance" would somehow reflect on my friends. I asked whether the norm was to go out to the back of the church to process in or if we would simply come into the sanctuary from the sacristy. Annoyed, he told me to "follow the altar boys; *they* know what they're doing." As we left the sacristy, he vested in surplice and stole. He stopped me at the side of the pulpit as we passed it. The processional proceeded into the church, altar boys included. He told the people who I was, proceeded to lead the liturgy and, to my surprise, took the pulpit for the reading of the gospel. He told the people what the readings were about, made a couple of announcements, then stood aside, telling me again, not-so-*sotto-voce*, to keep it short. He left the sanctuary and I was allowed to continue the liturgy.

Himself? He waited in the sacristy to say that he didn't believe that the Mass was valid. I told him he was not at liberty to make such a decision. He declared that he was as educated as I and that he was as smart as I. It seemed sad to me that he would be so threatened by the likes of me, but the reputation of Jesuits does sometimes precede us, and not always in a healthy way. I think he must have been hurt along the way, but it was evidently important for me to be very careful. The pastor then went into the church proper to yell at the remaining twenty-five or so people who were greeting one another. His message—that there was to be silence in his church because it is a Catholic church, not a Protestant one. His announcement was met by a calm but forceful voice from the back of the church saying, "You're the problem in this parish." The ongoing situation seemed hopeless. I was especially saddened but strangely encouraged, too, by the eleven-year-old acolyte who told me "Don't let him get to you, father; he does that to everybody."

The people had been to the bishop to ask for another pastor. The bishop said that this man had already been rejected in another parish. He had no one else to put in this pastor's place and that he was banking on the fact that this well-educated and prayerful community could "handle him." It is not really a case of a pastor taking comfort in a legalistic approach to problem solving but perhaps something more pathological. The pendulum sometimes swings because of pathologies, I think. But this parish community is expected by the beleaguered bishop to do therapy, I suppose, and grow themselves through self-denial and self-sacrifice. This is not altogether unwise given the time and place of the "problem," but it does cause reflection on the need for constant reform among the clergy.

The funeral

The woman who cooked and took care of the kitchen in the Jesuit house at the University asked me to "do the funeral" for her mother-in-law. The older woman had within the year gotten sick and gone to a nursing facility fifty miles from her own home, but within the parish where her son and his family lived and worshipped. The mother did not recover, but died. Rather than bring her to her own distant parish for burial, since she had essentially lived the last year of her life in her son's parish, actually right near the family burial plot in the local Catholic cemetery, and since the mother had been suffering from Alzheimer's Disease, the family asked the pastor if she could be buried from their parish. "Yes," was the answer, "but I, the pastor, cannot do it because I am too busy. You can do this if you get a 'visiting priest'."

I was happy to be able to do this for the wonderful woman who had been such a friend and gracious help in the life of the Jesuit Community for quite a number years. She had been a nun for close to twenty years before leaving the cloister and marrying her husband. She was an extremely sweet, kind woman.

The funeral went well—except that before it began the pastor informed me that "the suppression of the Jesuits is long overdue." This he had surmised because I had come from teaching class and had to return to teaching class, an hour away from his church, and I had worn a brown tweed jacket instead of a black one. I basically ignored him by saying, "Oh, thank you, Father." He was sufficiently surprised by that; he didn't keep flustering me before the funeral began. But he waited in the sacristy, busy as he was, and informed me afterward that the Mass was invalid and that the suppression, again, was long overdue. He repeated that phrase as though it were a practiced refrain, judged to be a quip of untold power and irony!

The problem with the "validity" of this funeral included a couple of pet peeves of his, which were not, since I'd never met him, even approaching my consciousness as possible problems for an overworked pastor. One difficulty was that I had allowed a fully-habited Immaculate Heart sister, a niece of the deceased, to read the epistle. Another, that I had left the sanctuary to wish peace to the family during the kiss of peace. He apologized to the altar boys for "having made you party to a mortal sin." Sadly, again, the altar boys made me aware that this was not directed at me so much as at everyone in general. Even more sadly, the funeral director apologized for the behavior of the pastor, because he had become a legend among the local funeral directors. This director, without any word from me, knew that something must have happened in the sacristy and apologized without a single word of explanation. Again, a whole community is subject to the personal law, not to say whim, of a difficult personality, who is the fully approved "overseer." The people seem somewhat victimized, but what could be the solution?

A consideration

These three stories have certain funny elements. However, I am a priest in good standing; how much more power do these men have over the people of God under their care. A sad state and not uncommon, nor unknown, nor, perhaps, is it a fully preventable circumstance. But the reflection these stories evoke further demands a basic explanation. How is it that this behavior arises within the Church where the very model of priesthood is the most kind and gracious, self-effacing and self-emptying Lord, Jesus, the Christ? How does such behavior continue and even thrive in the Church whose clarion is to love God above all and to love your neighbor as yourself?

The reflection and some further thoughts on how to grow less prone to control and more given to graciousness are the reasons behind the writing of this presumptuous essay. I would hope to point out a couple of principles to guide those young people who are called to service (*diakonia*) within the Church (*ecclesia*) according to the order of the High Priest, Melchizedek (from the Epistle to the

Hebrews and the ordination rite), as Jesus calls his disciples on Holy Thursday, to service of the Faith. We must all participate in Jesus' mission. The priesthood of Melchizedek is not contradictory of the priesthood of Aaron, but contrary in this sense. The motivation of the priest/king of Salem, unknown to the readers of *Genesis* but obviously worthy of Patriarch Abraham's abject and profound respect and reverence, was to *serve* these foreigners, Abram and Sarai. The motivation of the Levites, according to all the rules and regulations of the Pentateuch, is to serve God, in ritual purity and strictly adhering to the rules. There has grown a double function in the history of the People of God. How to reconcile the two is a matter for study and prayer.

It is important to admit, at this point, that the stories I have just related are not the only kind of story in my past. I have had wonderful experiences with other priests in other parishes where I was a visitor, experiences wherein I felt warmly admitted to the brotherhood of priests, shown professional courtesy and fraternal care. The presumption that I am a good man, ordained for God's service, fills me often with gratitude and an immediate awareness that this brother-priest and I are serving the same Friend. This is the kind of experience I wish all of us to share. It is the kind of experience, which should be the norm among Christians.

Those three stories, common enough, simply lead me to wonder why there is such a difference, like two totally different mindsets, about the very meaning of priesthood. The rest of this consideration of two manifestations of priesthood is an attempt to see how both the authoritarian and the kindly approach have roots in our one tradition, the lines of the priesthood of Melchizedek, as colored in by the regulations for that of Aaron.

It is not that I abhor a conservative approach toward keeping true to the rules. Indeed, how else would there be possible the comfort of common practice reinforcing the universality of the one, holy, catholic, and apostolic Church? It is not my intention to imply a necessary mean spirit whenever the clergy project the rules, protect the Law, and preserve the order of things. I do believe that this particular kind of tough-love, spirited regulation only rises to the level of mean-spirited willfulness as an aberration along with the sense of privilege, which ordination engenders in many a humble and sinful man. Entitlement is an insidious privilege. The strength and meaning of the prerogatives of the cult priesthood is passed down from the time of Aaron himself. It must be hard-wired, a temptation in the very structure of cult worship itself. Not initially given to this misreading, the long-serving pastor might develop into the weary pastor. (Putting the best face on an unpleasant experience is a well-worn Irish way, basically, of putting up with it.) The persevering person often gets overused. There are so many pitfalls, aren't there? Prayer is so important to prevent unwitting collusion with the evil one after years of faithful service. Friendship is also very important to help the overworked reflect and survive the proclivities of their demanding flocks.

But that consideration belongs in a different book.

5

Responsorial Psalm

Taste and see the goodness of the Lord.

A first bounce

When the priest pays attention to the deepest part of himself, the part in contact with the Holy Spirit, what happens to his priesthood? Does it make him more obedient to the will of his superiors? Does it make him more rebellious, more happy, or less inclined to deal with the weaknesses of others? I wonder how many of us get to that deepest part.

Discernment

Where does the Holy Spirit lead the priest who is trying to be the holiest priest he can be? This is an engaging question and has always been somewhat double-edged. The reason? It might be found in Paul's *Letter to the Romans*. There he talks of freedom and the law in such a way as to confuse those who merely read him—or those who merely listen to excerpts read from the pulpit. But for those who take the scriptures to prayer, who meditate in such a way as to allow contact between the contemplator and God, there is deeper and deeper meaning. This is how a life of prayer works, after all; the Lord is continually reaching out, revealing more and more as the person "grows in the spiritual life." For a priest, then, this growth can lead to better obedience and, sometimes, to a freer read of the situation than his superiors might like. The challenge is to "discern the spirits," isn't it? The danger is to become so sure of one's own insight that he forces it onto all and sundry. This danger can come from any insight, but it has a special tyranny when the convinced person is committed to service of a community over which he presides. The difficulty is manifest in this: that the person who feels God's love can be easily caught by a lesser spirit and brought to inconsistent or even contradictory conclusions while still in the "afterglow" of prayer. One of the principles we often easily miss in a life of prayer is that one needs to *recognize when the graced experience ends*. This is one reason the great mystics recommend keeping a journal, so that we can plot the experience and our differing responses. It is after we have left the Presence, as it were, that our own or someone else's conclusions are drawn; sometimes those conclusions are faulty but we think of them as coming from God. This is how the evil one works, if we follow the insights of the great mystics, Ignatius of Loyola, Theresa of Avila, John of the Cross, Meister Eckhart, *et al.*

So, the priest, because he is in a position of standing ritually between the people and God, has a deeply dangerous calling. The more prayerful he becomes, the more self-assured, the more fodder he becomes for the disintegrating angels who would use him to destroy that which he loves. The priest, therefore, would be better off if he did not try meditating? Actually, there is a way that his life would be much simpler, because he could look to a well-structured hierarchical Church whose leaders are at least tempted to make all his decisions for him. It could be a very comfortable life. It would be the ancient life of an Aaronic priest without the troublesome, conscious conscience. But it would also be a tremendously sad loss of possibility for the Church! The priest in union with God can be a very holy person and a deeply supportive leader of ritual prayer for God's people. He can also lead them astray, or be led himself by powerful lesser lights within the community. A lot depends on the priest's union with God.

The fact is, I know nothing good living in me—living, that is, in my unspiritual self—for, though the will to do what is good is in me, the performance is not, with the result that instead of doing the good things I want to do, I carry out the sinful things I do not want. When I act against my will, then, it is not my true self doing it, but sin which lives in me. In short, it is I who with my reason serve the Law of God, and no less I who serve in my unspiritual self the law of sin. (*Rom.* 7: 10-20, 25)

This should give us pause, and, indeed, it does. There is prayer and there is law and they both have a role to play in the life of the priest. The priesthood of Aaron is all about law and the priesthood of Melchizedek is all about spirit. The two must coexist in the mind and heart of the priest in order that he might participate in the one priesthood of Christ. This is daunting, but neither is it without precedent nor promise of help from the Spirit.

I have found that my own most profound proof of doing God's will in ritual comes from people who tell me, on the one hand, that I helped them to pray during the sacramental liturgy—baptism, funeral, wedding, Eucharist, and on the other hand, say that I didn't "get in the way" while leading the prayer. This might sound like I am engaging in self-praise. There is a little of that, I'm sure and relatively ashamed of it; I could not have written this book to be of help, however, if I hadn't felt the hand of God working through my own hands, the voice of God working through my own words, at least once in a while. It is those profoundly humbling experiences which lead me to want to share God's bounteous blessing. I have felt in union and, even though I might be presiding, I could feel God's presence as I did when I was a child. The fact that others might feel it too, while I am presiding, is deeply and astoundingly precious. I do not want to think that I am God's prophet; indeed, at those moments I have nothing to say. If I do talk it is to say, let us bask in God's love.

So, the proof that I should write this book is not that I know what I am doing, but that I have felt God doing what God does. I have also felt God say that I should share these insights, so I do. There can't be another response, God help us, than yes for me, at least eventually. When St. Theresa of Avila was suggesting that her sisters find a good spiritual director, she observed that it would be better to find a smart one than a holy one. When seeking help in discernment, it is better to have all the help we can get, in order to understand God and to respond. She indicates that being holy demands not only basking in God's presence, but in finding out what is of God and what is of something else when I am being "led" to do things. The work of discernment, then, is difficult enough, but necessary; without it we can all be led to perfidy.

6

A Second Reading

Some exegesis is necessary before homily writing.

In the very earliest experience of the "Chosen People," Abraham meets with a priest, Melchizedek. This is the first priest of the Israelites' communal experience of God; it occurs in a ritual of respect for the "guest-friend," who is a stranger. This was a consistent custom throughout the ancient world, sacred in its practice. Its omission was taboo.

Melchizedek, the king of Salem, brought out bread and wine and, being a priest of God Most High, he blessed Abram with these words:

> *Blessed be Abram by God Most High,*
> *The creator of Heaven and earth;*
> *And blessed be God Most High,*
> *Who delivered your foes into your hand.*

Then Abram gave him a tenth of everything. (*Genesis* 14:18-20).

This is the only mention of Melchizedek except for the psalm text (*Ps* 110: 4) in the Old Testament. In the New Testament he is described: "Without father, mother, or ancestry, without beginning of days or end of life, thus made to resemble the Son of God, he remains a priest forever" (*Hebrews* 7:3). This description is applied to Jesus.

The Deuteronomic history of priesthood, according to John Costelot, S.S., in the 1968 edition of the *Jerome Biblical Commentary* (pg. 707), is an early claim for the hegemony of Jerusalem over all the other priestly traditions in Palestine. Melchizedek becomes the very earliest priest of that city (non-existent as it was at the time of Abraham). Be that as it may, this Melchizedek is the priest to whom the Christ is compared by the writer of the *Letter to the Hebrews*; it is in this tradition that all priests are ordained in the Roman Catholic, western tradition. Jesus gives bread and wine, too, but this food and drink is, by His own sacramental admission and intervention, and expressed according to the inspiration of the writer of *Hebrews*, His very substance. The transubstantiated elements are what the ordained present in the liturgy to the People of God, food of angels for women and men. And so, the prototype/archetype is this self-emptying, self-giving priest-king, Jesus, prefigured at the very beginning of the whole story of salvation in Melchizedek, who also offered bread and wine——to Abram and Sarai.

...and then

The other tradition and *proto-image* of priesthood comes a little later. Later, in *Exodus* 4, Aaron, the Levite and brother of Moses, is named by Yahweh as the spokesperson, as it were, for Moses, who had complained to Yahweh that he was not good at words. Later still, after the leaving of Egypt and the planning for the future ritual life of the people of the Covenant, in *Exodus* 28, Yahweh establishes the cult priesthood of Aaron the Levite and his sons. "From among the Israelites have your brother Aaron, together with his sons Nadab, Abihu, Eleazar, and Ithamar, brought to you that they may be my priests." This group will be the priests for the cult of worship around

the Ark of the Covenant in perpetuity. In *I Chronicles* 24ff, the orders of Aaron's sons and the orders of Levi's sons receive classifica-
tion and a description of duties and rights. In *I Chronicles* 25, 26 the
duties of porters, cantors, and treasurers, as it were, for the ancient
rites of the Old Covenant, are set up.

... and then what?

Later still the tradition develops wherein the redactors, the Yah-
wist, Eloihist, Deuteronomic, and Priestly (J, E, D, and P) editors,
arrange the way the books are read, so that certain truths become
more, sometimes less, evident. For instance, we find that God does
not need a temple to speak to us and only a few lines later realize that
God demands a temple (*I Chronicles* 28:3-6) or there is really no
need for the People of God to have a king and then God demands
one (*I Samuel* 8: 7-9, *I Samuel* 9:15-17). God is overwhelmingly in-
sulted and will destroy His people and then He is tenderly telling
them through the prophet that He will protect them from their enemies (*I Chronicles* 21:7-17) and He will redress His own emotional
wounds and forgive us for whatever intolerable thing we might have
done (*Numbers* 14, *Exodus* 32, 34).

The proclivity of the people for sin is a problem to which the
priests of the Covenant, even after the golden calf incident, are not
immune, and so there are laws governing almost everything about
the way the ritual of ordination will be conducted (*Leviticus* 8, *Exodus* 29), the way the priests will dress (*Exodus* 28, 39), the way the
rules will be kept about sacrificial offerings (*Numbers* 15), ritual
meals (*Leviticus* 3-7, 22-24), the Meal of the Covenant (*Exodus* 34),
care of the utensils (*Exodus* 30), the structure of the temple (*Exodus*
25-27, 40), care of the sanctuary (*Exodus* 35-38), and so on.

There is a second set of priests of the tribe of Levi who are to
be given "...to Aaron and his sons as 'oblates'; they are to be given
to him by the sons of Israel." (*Numbers* 3:9,10) The rest of Numbers

3 and 4 covers the different delegated duties of the sons of the three sons of Levi.

...and then, now

All of the Deuteronomic and Levitical prescriptions and pro-scriptions establish a whole way of life for the priests of Aaron and for the Levites, whose duties become separated from those of the priests of Aaron, who alone might approach the Ark of the Covenant itself. Ultimately separate orders arose for the priests who entered the Holy of Holies and those who could only approach it.

A similar tradition exists in the medieval developments of the Christian cult priests. Sub-deacons, Deacons, Arch-deacons, Dea-conesses, Lectors, Acolytes, Porters, Exorcists, Priests, Archpriests, Right Reverend, Very Reverend, and Most Reverend Monsignori, Bishops, Metropolitans, Archbishops all develop over the centuries, with ordinations and offices, consecrations and rules. Then too, there are Abbots, Abbesses, Rectors, Priors, Prioresses, Reverend Moth-ers and Fathers General, Popes, Patriarchs, and Cardinals. The dif-ferent roles have had different rules. Some might think of all of this as a byzantine structure, and so it was, is, and may be forever.

These structures and the rules that govern them have a lot to do with a human need to provide guidance toward self-control and a systemic need which develops in the body politic for public control of private persons with privileged positions and entitlements. But the priest is not ordained according to the Order of Aaron or Levi. He is "...ordained 'a priest forever' according to the Order of Melchizedek." This makes all the difference in how he must order his own priorities. Sometimes it means he must go against the grain, sometimes he must cross the cultural norms because he is ordained according to a higher order, the order of the counter-cultural priest-hood of Christ. This priesthood of Christ, the priesthood of Melchizedek, demands of the ordained that, like the prototype or the *monotype*, as *Hebrews* would have it, with only one High Priest, the

Christ, in whose priesthood we all participate, demands of him that he pour himself out. He must pour his very substance into being for God's people, a servant, "a man for others" in the immortal phrase of Pedro Arrupe, beloved, former Father General of the Society of Jesus. The priest gives the bread and wine which becomes the Christ and which is manufactured by human hands, and still represents his own self as well as the rest of the People of God. At the Minor Elevation, before the consecration in the Eucharist, the bread and wine are offered to God, "Blessed are You, Lord God *(Beruch ato Adonai),* King of the Universe for You have given us this bread [and wine] to eat [and drink], fruit of the earth and the work of human hands; it will become our spiritual food [and drink]." This is why, after all, any of us has, from the twelfth century onward, willingly accepted the discipline of celibacy, because the totality of the gift makes sense. Even if we falter in the completion of that giving, the Christ of the consecration is the One who presides at the Feast.

And so...

We have two orders of priesthood in the Roman Church, embodied in the single men who are ordained. By "orders" here we are not speaking of the Rules of religious orders, like the Augustinians, Benedictines, Carmelites, Franciscans, Dominicans, or Jesuits, but of the "orders" of ordination in the Church and according to the rules of the Church. The priesthood "according to the order of Melchizedek," by which phrase every priest is called to ordination, suggests the total *pleroma,* like Christ's, according to Paul, an "outpouring" of the very self into the life's work of the priest. The cult priesthood, according to Canon Law, conversely, a "priesthood of Aaron" in effect, demands absolute adherence to the rules of behavior for all Christians and more absolute adherence to the rules for the clergy. The double meaning, the two understandings, sometimes come into conflict.

Thank God for the liberating, if confusing, canonical concept of *epieikeia* (or *epikeia*) which expects the priest, the bishop, the layperson to use an interior higher common sense when applying the law. Thank God, too, for the canonical concept of applying the more lenient reading to law whenever there is contention about how to understand an uncertain application of law. Be those canonical prerogatives as they may, the person, ordained or otherwise, is expected to follow a well-formed conscience rather than merely obeying a law when it reads counter to the interior law of love, learned in prayer in union with God and in consideration of the Tradition, by the gracious action of the Holy Spirit. Sometimes, this adherence to an interior code calls for heroism. More often, in the daily life of the Church, it calls for tender common sense. The ordained is expected to bear both yokes lightly, giving freely of what he has been freely given. In the "clash of uncoordinated orders" (a phrase borrowed from the work of Rudolph Arnheim, concerning taste in art, and particularly about buildings, in *The Dynamics of Architectural Form*, U. Cal. Press 1977) the priest often finds the need for prayer and discernment, and in this he is often left to seek a foothold in something larger than himself. The trick is to be sure that the foothold is on one of God's "footstools"! The examination of a foothold resting on a footstool, which rests, furthermore and ultimately, on another footstool at the foot of *the* Other, is the essence of discernment. The priest needs to be a man of prayer if he is to find a peace wholly within himself for himself and for "his" people, those given him by Father God and Mother Church. That holy peace, then, will have its place at the footstool, as it were, of the Heart of Christ, in his own heart.

7

Second Reading Again

The training that we received in seminary during my years there included precious moments wherein a professor would remind us that the call to priesthood is double-edged. Any question that this "call" would be just to do a job is rendered moot by the discussion of its double origin.

On the one hand, we should remember that we are called by the "People of God" to preside for them at the prayer services of the Church. This vocation to priesthood for and from the people is not usually considered the candidate's foremost spiritual or conceptual mandate. We are more often made aware of some inner drive, some relationship with the divine wherein we will find our own salvation. The idea, however, that we are called by the people of God makes us aware that the privilege is afforded to very few of the people. There is, consequently, a way in which we must deserve trust. The priesthood conferred on Aaron and his progeny by Yahweh Himself, in the Mosaic story in *Exodus* is the prototype for this priesthood. The deserving is granted by birth and rebirth in baptism. We need an analogous deserving, however, among our peers. There is a cultic place within the population reserved for the ones *allowed* to perform the rites of religion, *allowed* to speak for the people to the God of the

Whirlwind, the Earthquake, and the Fire. In other words, there is a place for priests which is timeless; we know from looking at other religious traditions including the Hebraic one, it is analogously prevalent in all religious cultures. This call to the cultic priesthood is tantamount to the call of the shaman, the witch doctor, the bonze, and the high lama. It is one that comes from God through the people *(and the people?)*; and so, there is a connotation of *ritual purity,* which demands that the priests live *up to code* to be worthy of continuance in the eyes of the people. The very nature of this call to the Aaronic priesthood is replete with Judaic requirements akin to those of the levitical priesthood. Aaron was the brother of Moses, called by Yahweh God to father an hereditary priesthood. Later the Book of *Leviticus* records all the rules for right representation of the vocations of both the "sons of Aaron" and the "sons of Levi." There is still a sense of Old Testament evaluation in the way that the people look at their priests and deacons.

Young priests, deacons, and students for the priesthood come up against those evaluative glances very soon. Everybody is a judge, it seems sometimes. Some of the glances come from family, some from friends, some from complete strangers, and some come in the mirror. We have righteous expectations of our priests. The trouble with those expectations is that there is no way that a single person could avoid stepping on somebody's expectations sometime in his life. This makes for a priesthood prone, perhaps, to self-doubt. The desire to counter or control the guilt or the doubt often finds the priest clinging to ritual purity as his *raison d'être;* he finds something akin to *keeping kosher* as a way to assuage the realization that he is not quite a perfect sacrificial lamb. This can lead to lots of trouble for the priest and for the ones he serves.

On the other hand, however, we are "ordained according to the order of Melchizedek." This priesthood is, again, quite different in origin from the Aaronic priesthood or that of the Levites. Melchizedek was a mythical priest/king who came from a non-existent kingdom to minister to the needs of Abram and Sarai when they were wandering in the desert. The authority of Melchizedek comes not from the people but from his mythical birthright. He is born to serve. This priesthood is the one that the writer of *Hebrews* claims for Jesus. He is our High Priest, the One whose singular priesthood we are called to imitate. What a glorious conception! This priesthood calls on us to rely on Jesus and on His saving grace, His birthright as it were, the scriptural origins bathed in mystery.

The call to priesthood, then, becomes a liberating thing. The consideration that all the work of salvation has already been done makes the priest's need for ritual purity much less important. Not unimportant, just less important, because the requirement for this priesthood is to serve the needs of the people, as Jesus did.

The whole of Paul's *Epistle to the Romans* touches on this kind of engaged freedom from the Law. Because salvation depends on Jesus, the purity of the priest is not a qualifier of the reality of Redemption. In one of the oldest theological traditions, which accounts for the dichotomy between the priest and the priest's work, the work of the Eucharist is done "*ex opere operato,*" (by the doing of the work, literally from the work having been worked) rather than "*ex opere operantis,*" (by the doing of the doer). This priesthood requires a constant attempt on the part of the ordained to be in union with Jesus, to be interiorly free because of His love. This is a wholly other and completely different understanding of priesthood than the Levitical understanding, which puts so much emphasis on the quality of adherence to external expectations in the performance of ritual.

The two understandings must go hand-in-hand, nonetheless, in the practice of priesthood within our historical and radically human context. The vicissitudes of culture, history, church politics, social expectations, and the like make even the idea of complete freedom (to do anything, anywhere, at any time), into shadows cast by candles, constantly changing and without discernibly distinct definition. The practice of the priesthood within our present *Sitz im Leben* (a phrase from biblical scholars meaning "life situation," as reference or backdrop, to understanding Sacred Scripture) demands both adherence to the rules of membership, as regulated by the Church in time and space, **and** the ability to make free gifts of service in God's name. Jesus' own priesthood was tempered by the society in which He lived and grew, tempered "even to death, death on a cross." (*Philippians* 2: 8)

There is a certain handicap in trying to be both upright according to human rules and free according to God's grace. This essay is, again, an attempt to suggest ways that the priest must keep his head and his heart both working in the completion of his ritual duties. He must serve like Melchizedek, or indeed like the Lord Himself, and yet he must keep the will of the Church close to his heart. So he must use his gifts, the ones which he alone brings to this vocation, to be the freest *and* most true priest he can be.

The following suggestions are from one priest's experience. I hope to help other priests and deacons to be true to their two-sided, double-edged call. However, the best tool, aside from prayer, for being able to differentiate between the two roles called into play is knowledge. To know some psychology, philosophy, and theology is the ground of our seminary training. To put them together in good practice of the profession demands a great knowledge of the liturgies of the Church. The history can be read and studied. Josef Jungmann SJ is just one, albeit, in the estimation of many historians, the most important chronicler of the history of the liturgy, but there are many. The job of knowing about liturgy is a life's work; prayer and study are still called for, even after ordination.

That the little round "host" has been used only since the development of the monstrance in the Carolingian court, or that the altar rail is a medieval development devised to separate the property of the feudal liege lord from that of the Church, or that the organ was not part of church music until well after the beginning of the second millennium, are important pieces of information which free the priest to help the people in their worship. Many of the faithful believe that whatever was present in the church of their youth was always there. Just knowing that neither the crucifix nor the gentle human Virgin regularly resided in the great churches virtually until the second millennium is an awareness of tremendous importance. The first millennium had images of the *Theotokos*, the Mother of God, the Virgin *Orans*, the Good Shepherd, the Lamb of God, the Last Supper, the Last Judgment, and the empty cross of the Risen Christ. There is so much to know! Information frees the mind a little more to be more open to the motivations of the Spirit. This is an important purpose of seminary training, to know that there is much more to learn and that there are available sources for a life of delving deeper.

Many are noticing of late, however, a tendency in the newly ordained to think of their role as that of protector of the traditions, as servants of the central curia of the Vatican, as priests ordained to keep the people of God in line.

Knowledge should help the priest to explain where traditions come from and what they mean. It should also help the priest become less worried about kosher praxis of human traditions while he becomes more cognizant of the miraculous work of the Holy Spirit in the prayer life of the People of God, in the *prayer work of the people of God* (the etymological meaning of *leitourgia*, liturgy). He becomes more reverent toward the self-disclosing, self-emptying, constantly-renewing acts of the Christ. He becomes more God-fearing when he approaches the altar to praise the Father—correlatively, we can hope, with less human respect.

Grounding the Reconciliation

The challenge to be both the Aaronic priest and the Melchizedekian one is formidable not because the ideas are hard to grasp but because of the contrary directions in which the "devotees" travel. There is a kind of Apollonian/Dionysian dichotomy here. Remember how Nietzche pointed out the difference in the way the two Greek gods model creativity for us? The two positive drives display different devices of priestly attitude.

There is in Hindu culture the vast difference between the preserver and destroyer gods, Vishnu and Shiva; they are, ironically for us, two of the three major deities in the Hindu pantheon existing in irenic iconographical balance. Along with Brahma, the creator, they are the triune godhead, the most important of all the vast array. At any rate, the consideration of the conflict of contrary directions in religious systems has reverberations in most religious traditions, including the Judeo-Christian. Two ways of leading the people to prayer must not, however, bifurcate the role or the heart of the priest.

The contraries work themselves out into two basic attitudes for the Catholic priest, which seem to motivate our clergy everywhere. One is either a stern reminder of what must be done to please God

69

or a nurturing one, which recognizes the work of the Spirit in all persons. Problems arise, of course, when one is unable to recognize the two contraries and, thus, cannot reconcile them in himself. The people need priests who are aware of both motivations. More, the Lord needs priests who are reconciled within themselves, because such reconciliation or balance of contraries is necessary to the health of all of God's creation. So, even though one might seem to be more authoritarian, he must actually have the ability to display a good heart. Even though one seems to accept everyone as they are, he must be able to say what needs to be said.

This reconciliation within the self is the duty and goal of all human spiritual life. One loves like God when one is both clear about what is good or right and kind in rendering the ritual services we are called to offer—strong and tender! It also helps to differentiate between great matters and small.

A priest is called upon to be presider at many different kinds of ceremony which mark the coming and going of God's people on the earth. There has arisen a new requirement for the priest—to perform, while "on stage," new now because, for the last few hundred years, the priest had been mostly facing away from the congregation. The sacred rites were performed in a kind of hidden or secret way, in an ancient language. What happened in the Western Rite was akin to what still happens in the Eastern Rites. The eucharistic ritual was performed in the presence of the congregation but not openly. In the East the iconostasis covers most of what happens during the eucharistic liturgy. In the East there is the *iconostasis;* in the West there are the corporal, the humeral veil, the communion rail, the rood screen—all ways to help the congregation keep its distance while the sacred and secret ritual is conducted within the sacred precincts, the *holy of holies,* more or less, as in the Hebrew Temple of Solomon, behind the "veil of the temple." The old fiddle-back chasubles often had painted or embroidered panels depicting the mystery re-presented on the other side, in front of the priest. Now, however, after Vatican II and the placing of the altar right in the midst of the people, the priest's job is much more personally demanding. He must represent not only the Church's hierarchy to the people and the people themselves to God but also the ever-present Christ.

In Dom Odo Casel's wonderful conceptualization from the early decades of the twentieth century (*The Mysteries of Christian Worship*), the priest makes Christ present again, he *re-presents* Him, the Lord. So this wondrous phrase has the terrifying corollary that the priest must somehow "put on Christ" in a special way and for this special time. I think it more daunting now than it was in the recent past, before the Council. The priest must now be conscious that he stands face to face with Christ's disciples and must make Him more real through his own actions. This is the sacramental reality, of course, but there is, on the interactive human level, this new realization that the priest must act in such a way as to allow Jesus to be more present to His people—through his very own faulty self! The presence of Jesus doesn't depend in any way on how well the priest does this. In fact, this is not at all his responsibility. Although validity and liceity are traditionally determined by the intention of the priest, the Presence can take care of Itself. The priest's responsibility, however, is to go through the form and the words with intention. The underside of that particular coin contains this message: the priest can ruin it! He can conduct himself in such a way that the people are preoccupied with his performance more than they are with paying attention to the Lord, present among His people. This is a very bad thing to do.

So, how do we avoid it? How do we keep from getting in the way? The rest of this essay is a reflection on my own ways of trying to do both, being a son of Aaron, a levitical priest, the *presbyter* (elder or "the old one") and the focus of the Priesthood of Melchizedek, the *pontifex* (bridge builder), who empties himself into this communal participation in the Body of Christ. I hope my presumption that this would be helpful does not offend.

Cathedral Wedding: The New Order

I had spent quite a few hours with the young man all during his academic career; we'd had a strong relationship, but I did push him hard. We talked about many things—one was trying to help him deal with the possibility that his behavior, when "under the weather," was problematic. I knew he had a drinking problem which might be alcoholism because of certain signs which had become evident in my dealings with him and his fraternity brothers. I'd been the fraternity advisor for well over a decade and got to know a lot of the young men very well. We worked through the growing realization for years. Now it had come about that when he was to marry, a couple of years after graduation, I was honored to be asked to preside. He's doing so well and I am proud of him, very proud of him as a human being, a brother, and a person with a problem with which he is dealing. She knows and is willing to help him deal. They are a couple with great promise!

The wedding would take place in the local cathedral, where I had previously presided at a number of weddings for my young student friends as the official witness for the Universal Church and for the Commonwealth of Pennsylvania. They had all been nuptial masses and each one was unique; the couple I had come to know and love, each time, had gone through the meaning of the rituals within the rite. The wedding liturgies were unique reflections of the couples, and the fact that I seemed to be one of their friends usually made the guests happy that "the wedding was so personal and the couple seemed so involved."

The administration of the cathedral had changed its way of dealing with visiting priests, and the rector had become a bit of a tyrant. When we came to the place for the rehearsal, a most affable deacon, with whom I'd dealt before, informed me, "We'll do this our way; there are to be no variations from the norm; no wedding may be different from any other wedding, except for the readings." I was a bit shocked, and, though somewhat miffed, I figured, "when in Rome..." The couple was unhappy with the arrangement because so many of the things they'd planned had to be scrapped, such as who stood where, who would bring the gifts to the altar, etc. The rehearsal lasted an hour, and there were many don'ts proclaimed with absolute calm and firm kindness by the deacon. He was really very professional, as if he were the *maitre d'* at a restaurant; we both knew he was acting under orders.

There were a few arrangements which I myself found compromising. The reason why none of the readers could practice reading from this pulpit was "because it would take too much time." No discussion, just short-clipped orders from above, from the commandant of the church. The microphone would work very well, "Trust me. There is no lavaliere microphone for you; only the archbishop is allowed to use the lavaliere, and it is locked up by his secretary." I was assured that I could use the mike with the long cord, which would allow me complete access to half of the sanctuary. The other mike on the altar is very powerful but only has a very short cord and so cannot be used except at the altar itself (only after the liturgy did I realize that that altar mike was set up but hadn't been plugged in!). The tabernacle key (which would definitely be there—trust me) was missing, and so I had to hide the Eucharist under a corporal in front of the tabernacle until the end of Mass (they hadn't provided a chalice veil). This is no real difficulty, of course; this kind of thing happens all the time; we just deal with it. But the fact that so many things were left undone, making the cathedral seem really disorganized and ungracious to a visitor (at great expense to the couple for rental of the space and playing of the organ—they couldn't afford the singer) while seeming so official and efficient in dealing with us, is a surprising underbelly to the strictness of the rehearsal and the letters sent to the photographer and the couple beforehand. So many rules, so little care!

But the *really* problematic thing came for me when the deacon informed the bridal party that "Father will invite all those who are in communion with Rome and who are properly reconciled with the Universal Church to come to receive the Eucharist, if they have received the sacrament of penance in preparation within the last week." The whole tenor of the rehearsal had taken on the tone of us bad people coming to the center of the archdiocese to try to misuse their stuff. Considering that we were all imbeciles, we were perfectly willing, of course, to admit that the non-present-presider's will about all the little particulars must be adhered to absolutely. It was unpleasant trying to help the wedding party to feel good about it all. I did my best to imply that the cathedral staff was doing its best.

This attitude, that the unintelligent faithful must be led by the educated protectors of the teachings of the Magisterium and that the use of the Presbyterium must be rigorously conducted "according to Hoyle," can feel rather insulting in the execution. But more importantly, it reduces the priesthood of the laity to mere obedience. The idea that there can be no Eucharist under both species, except by special permission to the couple themselves, that there may be no other ministers of the Eucharist in order to preserve the necessary uniformity at all weddings witnessed in the cathedral, seems to deny the way in which this most important ritual in lay Catholics' lives could educate them to the place they should take in the life of the Universal Church, to use marriage as the prototype as YHWH God does, as Jesus does, as Paul does.

That is, of course, unless we have an undeniable and unswerving political reality, as presently we do; it insists that the role of the faithful is only to do as they are told. Lay people may interfere in the proper role of the ordained within the *"presbyterium," for*merly known as the "sanctuary," only by special and explicit privilege. This comes quite a distance from the place in which we stood at the beginning of life within the presbyterate! The privilege to which I am ordained is, in fact, also called into question when faced with the authority and power of some local pastors. How difficult it must be to be a mere layperson in these situations—with no recourse.

The priesthood of Melchizedek, the self-emptying fullness, which Paul describes as the *kenosis* of Christ, is not given much evidence in those pastorates which so carefully preserve their privileges and protect the prerogatives and duties of the priesthood of Aaron.

I wonder if, in the present situation, there is a way to think positively about the Second Vatican Council's documents on the liturgical life of the Church, the priesthood of the people, and the role of the laity, while affirming the norms which come insistently from the Vatican curia. There seems to be a marked and firm agreement in Rome that lay people, particularly women, are to be kept from any attempt to arrogate to themselves the prerogatives of the ordained. Especially reserved are the rights of those raised to the fullness of ordination to the episcopacy. It is becoming difficult to reconcile the authority of the teaching on which I was raised with the authority of the present documents which so limit the free expression of prayer on the part of the people; lay persons, permanent deacons, priests, and even bishops are expected to toe the line. No deviations from ritual purity in *praxis*, as established by *fiat* from Rome—will this make us more fully the people of God as envisioned in the documents of Vatican II, or indeed, in the Pauline epistles to the *Romans, Corinthians, Colossians*, and *Thessalonians?*

At any rate, I continue to reflect on my own experience of thirty-five years of priesthood and suggest that these reflections might help the thinking Church to adjust to the present teaching of the magisterial bodies and/or, in light of Augustine's understanding of the three-pronged *magisterium* or teaching authority of the Church (theologians, hierarchy, and the *sensus fidelium*), to help the pendulum to swing back toward the clarion call of John XXIII and Paul VI.

10

Ecclesia Mater

The title of this chapter on the meaning of tenderness in the practices of the priesthood comes from a story that my rector, Fr. Gene McCreesh, S.J., told me about his first days in the old Burma Mission, after World War II but before the expulsion of foreigners, when the country became Myanmar. There were some confusing things that came up in the normal course of his priesthood and in ritual life with his people. Gene was not quite sure, within the cultural context new to him, about some things people were asking him to do. He went to the Archbishop in Rangoon with his questions, wanting direction about how to handle a particular confusion. The niceties of Canon Law in one cultural context might read differently against the needs of the people in another. The archbishop's response was memorable and helpful to Gene. It became for him a paradigm of missionary practice. He quoted it to me and others often, in the hope that it might help us deal with difficulties in dealing with students, staff, and faculty in the university where I had just begun a career as a member of the Arts faculty and as a Jesuit priest living in the student residence system. "*Ecclesia Mater* [The Church is a Mother], Father; do what you have to do," is what the archbishop so eloquently prescribed as a rule of thumb for the laborer in the field. It has a certain charm and the power of a *koan*; repetition of the phrase gives me a sense of how the apostle must respond to his flock. I should think this parable would encourage any worker in the field to trust his/her own inclination to kindness, looking up the requirements as loving backdrop to a first response in tenderness. This advice was, of course, originally given in the context of the apostolate of the foreign missions before Vatican Council II and under the shadow of the old Code of Canon Law, with its famous "*epikeia* clause," in effect. That canonical insight gave the same kind of leeway to the priests who would help the faithful to get what they needed from the Church. It has its counterpart in the present Code. There is another canon which says that if there were a discrepancy about the application of law, the more lenient understanding should prevail. The law seems to have encouraged a sense of freedom, like that spoken of by St. Paul in the *Epistle to the Romans*, a freedom to act according to a higher law of love, which we know from studying the heart of the Christ, from knowing it intimately.

There has been a swing to the right in respect to the advisability of allowing the ordained to think so freely or to take the authority of the hierarchy so personally in hand. The idea still, however, has some *caché* within the confines of hearts old enough or well-read enough to remember or able to find the underpinnings of an older dispensation. The consequence of an understandable caution could, on occasion, express itself in a kind of fearful scrupulosity and a reluctance to take risks. Those risks, after all, might make the cleric seem, horror of horrors, to have made a mistake. A mistake might expose him as blameworthy in front of a more authoritative arm of the Church. The ordinary *magisterium* is given the cloak and dagger of the Renaissance Inquisition. This is not a fortunate development, ambulatory when it occurs.

Be my hands

When the faithful come up against a fearful clergyman who will not take any risks to help them accomplish what they feel they must do in their own attention to the mind of God in their lives, they might respond to him with acrimonious displeasure or they might over-react—to their own loss. If the response to their perceived needs contains threats to their own well-being or that of their families, they can feel victimized. The response can be, in the face of a recalcitrant clergyman with non-negotiable power over their ritual life, extreme, to say the least. That would be a very sorry outcome from this understandable caution in the exercise of the priestly ministry, wouldn't it? People have left the Church in the past because of "irreconcilable differences." Some of those differences are now being reconciled after generations of separation (through inter-religious dialogues, for instance, between Roman Catholic leadership and the Lutheran Church and the member churches of the Anglican Communion as well as with the Orthodox Churches). There has been terrible fracturing of the Body of Christ in global communions. It should not happen again, please God. But on the interpersonal level, fracture could be foresworn by a little forbearance.

It is specifically in the carrying out of our priestly ministry that we priests can be the hands of Christ. Remember that image often used by Archbishop Fulton Sheen, wherein the handless statue of the Sacred Heart was the only thing left standing in a ruined cathedral in the post-World War II wreckage of Europe? It seems that some thoughtful GI, in the archbishop's famous story, had handwritten a poster placed before the statue. It said simply, "You must be my hands," a reprise of the famous prayer of St. Theresa of Avila. The archbishop used that story often in describing the *diakonia* of the Church, the call to serve. As he put it, we **must** help one another. This is the meaning of Jesus' double commandment to all of us.

Many of the faithful, brought up on such stories, have the idea that we all participate in the salvific priesthood of Christ. The *Epis-*

tle to the Hebrews has taken hold of their hearts and they feel called to act in His name. It is discouraging to find a cautious-hearted priest who will not help us to celebrate the birth of a child, the death of a parent, or marriage to a beloved spouse in a way that fits the special needs of this particular family, while complying with the require- ments of the universal Church. Of course, sometimes the request is inappropriate, but too often it is by only a little stretch of the norms that we could help the faithful so much. The response of the too cau- tious is, too often, to say nothing other than "this is not done!" In their own estimation those faithful people feel unloved and misun- derstood, while they feel judged as "disloyal," for even asking such a favor. They lose heart and sometimes lose hope in the Church.

A story to make the point. A few years ago one of my priest di- rectees (coming to me for spiritual direction) told me of his annoy- ance at a couple coming to ask to be married in the Church. The "couple" in this instance was a young woman and her father asking that she and her "room-mate" boyfriend of a few years be united in holy wedlock. My friend told her that they were living in sin and that he would not consider marrying them unless she moved back in with her mother. I asked if he wanted me to respond to his story. He said he guessed that's why he was telling me (this happens often in spiritual direction). I said I thought he was an SOB for not realiz- ing that this was a time of grace, of great possibility in the ecclesial life of this couple, finally growing up to a sacramental commitment and he was putting up roadblocks. He saw my point and asked what I thought he should do. I suggested "biting the bullet," calling the young woman, apologizing, removing his obstacles, and asking to meet with the couple. He actually did that. Everything seems to have worked out fine. But imagine what wisdom and extreme balance would have been required for this couple and the father to remain open to that priest—or, more darkly, to the whole Church! Think, too, what a wonderful example the recalcitrant priest became!

If, indeed, the Church is a mother, then the best mothers we know should be the image for us of how she, through our ministry, would treat her children. This must demand some soul-searching on the part of the priest, but all of us should know at least one mother who epitomizes what the Church should do. The Virgin Mary, for one, became, in the second millennium, the very image we seek. In the first millennium, she was often conflated with the Church as the *hodegetria*, pointing to the Son, the woman seated on the throne of Solomon, the "seat of wisdom," or the *orans* figure, praying with arms outstretched for all the faithful.

In the nineteenth century, Louis de Montfort articulated her status as the "mediatrix of all grace." Mary does for all what the Church sacraments do for some. The Virgin becomes powerful in our minds and hearts both as person and as symbol. John, on the Island of Patmos, had a vision of her as the very symbol of the Church, the woman clothed with the sun, crowned with twelve stars, and standing on the moon, pregnant with the Second Coming (*Revelation* 12), in danger but under the protection of angels and mythical beasts.

So, what can this mean, the Church as Mother, in the context of us priests trying to serve the faithful? Does it not mean that we should rejoice with, weep with, live with, the faithful? I propose that this living with the faithful demands a complete entering-in, an "incarnation," if you will. Similar to the outpouring, the *kenosis* of Jesus, according to St. Paul, we must pour ourselves into the sacramental lives of those who approach us to ritualize their encounter with God. We owe it to them and, even more, we owe it to the Master to do our best to be His hands in the situation, to **be** "the woman clothed with the sun."

A bit of history

The "Cult of the Virgin" is mostly a second millennium phenomenon. The Mother of God (as defined at the Council of Ephesus in 431) was revered because of her relationship to the Christ. She was the prototype of the perfect follower of Christ; she became the image of the Church. In early iconography she stood to pray with her hands outstretched in the *orans* position. She sat on the chair of Solomon, the "seat of wisdom," becoming a *type* of Wisdom within the Church. In Byzantine iconography she had a large head, to hold her wisdom. She often was found within a *vesica piscis*, the fish- or almond-shaped intersection of two circles, later called the *mandorla* (Italian for almond), a frame usually reserved for only the Christ or the Mother of God. The intersection of the two circles proclaims the union of earth and heaven, Jesus come to earth through the co-operation of His mother with God's grace.

The second millennium brought not only a new iconographic interest in the Christ on the cross (as opposed to the Christ in Last Judgment, as the Good Shepherd, and at the Last Supper) but also in the maternal relationship of the Queen of Heaven with her subjects, or of the earthly Mother of Jesus with her Son. In the Romanesque and Gothic artistic eras, the personality of the Mother of God developed. She took on more humanistic qualities. The *"Belle Verriere,"* the miraculous blue virgin of the oldest glass in the south ambulatory wall of the cathedral of Chartres, austere and hieratic, gave way to the smiling, sibilant Notre Dame of Paris. Her head became more like those of other characters, her interaction with the baby became much less hieratic and heraldic, and more naturally interactive. She stood up in the manner of a mother standing with her child on her hip; in s-curved statues and illuminations, she became the harbinger of elegance. She was also depicted more and more in the stories of the preaching and mendicant orders, in the Childhood narratives and the Stations of the Cross. Devotion through pilgrimage and the rosary made Mary more one of ours, more one of us who has made it, more prime intercessor, more mother with access to the Throne of God and nurturer of God Himself, *Theotokos.*

Henry Adams, in *Mont Saint Michel and Chartres,* gives us an understanding of courtly love and courteous behavior as envisioned by Eleanor of Aquitaine and her daughters. We get an impression of how the medieval mind addressed power at court and recognize the developing role of the *Theotokos,* as Queen in God's heavenly court.

Crowns start showing up all over the known world. Cimabue, Giotto, and Duccio rendered her more human but kept the nobility. Bellini and Caravaggio made her Italian. Rubens, Belgian; Rembrandt and van Dyke, Dutch; Murillo, Spanish; Riemenschneider and Pacher, German; Rublev, Russian. By the full flowering of the Renaissance, her depictions exhibited ethnic and national traits everywhere. In the "new world" the Virgin of Guadalupe is Mayan, Cuapa is Nicaraguan, Cartago is Costa Rican; the Virgin is ours, and we rely on her.

The idea that she was immaculately conceived, free of the human trials resultant from original sin, became a *leitmotif*; her face did not age, she did not feel the pangs of childbirth, she never felt anger, pain, or sorrow. The prime example would be the face of Mary in Michelangelo's earliest Pietà, now in Saint Peter's Basilica, the Bruges Madonna, and the Medici Madonna. It is the same face: young, vibrant, somewhat undisturbed in her holiness, at both the beginning and the end of Jesus' life. It is, of course, counter to evangelical and patristic histories and later Mariology. This is, however, where we see the *cult* developing.

Cult of the Virgin < = > "Divine Quaternity"

Carl Jung describes what has happened to the understanding of Mary in this development against the backdrop of his "collective unconscious" which relies on "archetypes"—universalized human subconscious or unconscious ways of dealing with what we need to comprehend in order to make sense out of our conscious life. He says that the need for balance between *animus* and *anima* archetypes demands a balance in the subconscious reading of the revelation of the Trinity. According to this psychodynamic theory, Mary becomes the psychological/archetypal fourth member of the "divine quaternity." This is, to be sure, a very subtle psychological discussion, not proposed as doctrine but suggested as psychological grounding for images of wholeness; it also gives a credible explanation for the development of the cult. Accordingly, Mary "rounds out," as it were, the relative imbalance of the Holy Trinity, with the Father and Son being images of the male principle, the *animus*, and the Holy Spirit representing the feminine principle, the *anima*. Again, this is not theology but psychology. It does bear further study to come to a better understanding of how the cult developed.

Thus, the image of Mary as not only prime example of the Christian, but also as the major maternal intercessor before God, motivates a gentle image of the Church——counter to the power-broker Church of Western Christendom, with armies vying to control the throne of Peter.

So what about the Priesthood?

Much more could be said about the cult of the virgin. For our purposes here, however, it is sufficient to note that the development of reverence for the Mother of God is multi-faceted and has a long history. For the priest, it is good to be aware of the different images, because the idea of Mary as image of the Church has repercussions in the way that we see the Church as Mother, *ecclesia mater*.

In the papal encyclical *Mater et Magistra,* Pope John XXIII develops this image with his own take on the double role of the Church, as mother and teacher. This is one of the underpinnings, therefore, at the beginning, the initial thrust, of Vatican II. It bears contemplation that the idea of Church as mother was in the mind of John XXIII as he moved toward the sea change which had visible waves long after the close of his and his successor's Vatican Council II.

According to Adolphe Tanquercy, (*A Manual of Dogmatic Theology*, transl. by Rev. Msgr. John J. Byrnes, Desclee, New York, 1959, pp. 176-182), "The *ordinary* and *universal* magisterium is that which is carried on daily through the continuous preaching of the Church among all peoples. It includes: 1. The preaching and proclamations of the Corporate Body of Bishops, 2. universal custom or practice associated with dogma, 3. the consensus or agreement of the Fathers and of the Theologians, 4. the common or general understanding of the faithful."

In a *Commonweal* article Archbishop Weakland noted before the turn of the millennium that Paul VI had capitalized *magisterium*. He noted that the change allowed Augustine's three-pronged understanding of the teaching authority of the Church, hierarchy/theologians/*sensus fidelium*, to become a single entity in the minds of centrists in the Curia. The *Magisterium* became the teaching authority residing primarily in the pope. The article is convincing in its suggesting concern.

It is, almost necessarily, confusing for the bishop/priest/deacon of the post Vatican II world to see conflicting messages about his role. The task is to internally conflate two divergent motivations. I believe that, with much prayer and trust in the Holy Spirit, we will develop a whole new theory of priesthood for the third millennium as well as a whole new understanding of the role of Mary in the divine economy. On the threshold of God's new world we need not be afraid.

The encyclical *Deus Caritas Est* of Pope Benedict XVI is brimming with tenderness. He speaks of the four loves, *eros* in constant interplay with *agape, philia* becoming possible between Christ Jesus and the Christian, and *caritas* as the fullness of *diakonia*, service in Christ's name. He takes the same words from Augustine as C.S. Lewis in *The Four Loves* and wraps them up in his understanding of who the Church is, the Bride of Christ, in response to the love of God. This is certainly a blessing in our day. It promises to inform the priesthood well into the future with this same attention to an inner demand for tenderness in all things.

Let us consider now, in the following chapters, some ways of conceiving the active conflation of the two roles, the two kinds of priesthood, in the sacramental life of the priest—of the Church.

11

Ordination

The church was old when I was a little boy kneeling in that dark space. Not too big, it was a kind of farm-community, frame building in Flushing, Queens, New York, built before the suburbanization of Long Island. I remember the beautiful marble statues inside, in front of the proscenium arch. I know now that they must have been Carrara marble—they were pure white, articulate, romantic not sentimental, larger than life, and powerful. The Virgin Mother especially caught my imagination. She had a crown, and her smile was engaging. Her Son, just younger than a toddler, was appealingly cute but serene. Like so many babies I have since baptized, giving the adults food for thought—this infant is recently come from the hand of God and s/he knows it! I found consolation in praying before that statue, even before first communion. I had no idolatrous impression that that stone statue was a person, but it did help me to focus on one or two.

There was a large crucifix at the edge of the sanctuary. I often wondered as a small child why there were so many crosses and crucifixes in the same place, my immature, obsessive-compulsive, neonatal or neophyte artist's mind demanding a clarity of number. But that crucifix, with its polychromy, bloody knees, glass eyes, and miniscule teeth, even though it was smaller than life-size, looked like one of us. It did connect me with a suffering Person beyond the sanctuary and the liturgy. Later encounters with the scholarship of Rudolph Otto (*The Idea of the Holy*), Josef Jungmann (*Missarum Solemnia*), H.W. Janson (*History of Art*), Carl Jung (*Man and His Symbols*), Mircea Eliade (*The Sacred and The Profane: Patterns In Comparative Religion*), Kenneth Clarke (the *Civilization* TV series) and others helped me to see how these figures were working on my spiritual imagination. Then, I was enthralled with the thoughts, feelings, and inner acts of devotion that these figures witnessed in me.

In those days of my personal "early church," the priests were privileged characters who alone were allowed to touch the sacred, with their fingers bent in that impossible Catholic *mudra* of forefinger and thumb on the right hand consecrated to God alone. They were worthy, in my memory still, of God's call. They were (all but one) kind, wise, manly but gentle, and very respectful of women (like the nuns and my Mom). There was a real sense that the Church was where God reigned. This is the Church to which I felt called.

It was full of romance, dignity, art, truth, respect. I wanted to help the crucified Lord to spread His message that God loves us and we should act accordingly. It all seemed so very simple then. I was aghast that people missed the point. I have since gotten older and, alas, wiser. The Church is full of people who want to get rid of other people's "crutches." I have found so much of the dignity and kindness gone as I have matured. In the main this seems so because the organic entity that was thriving in my childhood is mercilessly disenfranchised by those who think it their duty to keep others from pursuing religious values "less valid" than their own. These have lately become the harbingers of ritual purity; earlier they were the designers of a brand new understanding of Church. The motivation to righteousness seems healthy enough at first, but once it is reduced to a judgmental will to control all who are not privileged with certain insights and particular prerogatives, it deteriorates into unkindness and constant righteous indignation. This cannot be what priests aspire to when they first feel called by the Master. This is the "dark side" of the cultic priesthood. Martin Marty (*New York Times Magazine*, 30 September, 2001), talks about the basics of *fundamentalism*; this kind of will to control is a sign for him of that kind of fundamentalism which will not allow any insight into reality other than one's own.

This priest, born on another planet, as it were, has tried to keep focused, in the exercise of his office, on the love of God and the consequences of that love. With Vatican II and its aftermath there was a lot of helpful underpinning for the focus. In the sacraments, when we take the place of the Lord by saying the words or doing the deeds, we must help God's people to connect with that loving Lord. It must be that our task as priest is to do this by using the signs (the sacraments themselves) wrapped in symbolic language, movement, and images, to encourage the encounter—without getting in the way. This is a daunting task!

Indeed, the task is almost impossible, except for grace. I believe that grace comes to each of us according to our human gifts and frailties ("grace builds on nature"), so that being comfortable in our own skins before God and humans is the way that one best becomes the *presbyter*, the elder/priest, he is called to be.

The place that we hold as *pontifex*, the bridge-builder/priest, is the position given by the people of God whereby we are expected to use the wisdom of the Church, giving roost to the Holy Spirit, who acts within the sacramental life of the Church. We are to *connect with* the old ways, the old truths. The people expect us to know a lot of stuff, to be full of wisdom. We are not always up to their expectations. However, there is more than the call of the people in answer to which we take the place of the cultic priest.

I like to think of the "cultic priest" within the Catholic tradition as the successor to the sons of Aaron and the levitical priests who held the ritual role of leadership. But we are ordained "according to the order of Melchizedek," the mythical priest/king of Salem who visited Abram and Sarai in the desert, bringing them bread and wine from a not-yet-existent holy place. This, a "first Eucharist" of sorts, was a very gentle help given to our patriarch and matriarch to meet the grace of God. This mythical priest-king is our more important prototype, the one chosen by the Church itself, these many centuries, as she ordains us. The call to priesthood is, then, even in our ages-old ritual of ordination, a mythic call from God Himself to the individual man. The bishop "relies on the testimony of the Church" that the men presented for ordination are worthy of it. This is when, in the ordination ritual, the congregation indicates their vote of confidence by applauding. I remember the rush of awe when the thunderous applause of my family and the families of the eleven men ordained with me indicated that they thought we were ready and able. It was thrilling, romantic, dignified, tender. I remember being very happy at that moment, but knowing deep down that the call from the Lord was much more important than the call from humankind. Lucky for me, I had been given a pretty definite sense of being "chosen by God," through ten years of spiritual experience into which Jesuits are trained. I had, on that very day itself, a realization of the two priesthoods. I answered the cardinal's question: "I am ready and willing."

On the interior struggle for self-acceptance that my visceral experience of ordination required, let me just say that once, on retreat, I "heard" the voice of Jesus say, "I don't love you any more than I love anybody else." I was devastated for a moment, but I heard further, "your gift is that you know that I love you." This fact for me has empowered me all through my adult life; humbled, I realize that God loves us all so very much and I am supposed to help others realize what I have such a hard time realizing myself. It is a great part of my personal vocation. I think it is probably part of everyone's vocation, called to freedom by the salvific action of the Christ, freedom that allows us to enter into the lives of our faulty flock and do what we can for them, knowing that He loves them and is at work in their lives long before and long after we are. Even Peter said, "Depart from me, Lord, I am a sinful man." But the understanding Lord had other ideas for their relationship—and for ours.

The day of ordination itself is replete with visceral experiences. Nobody could forget the feelings of lying face down in the midst of the people he has known and loved most in the world, while they pray the litany for him. Nor could anyone forget the imposition of hands by the bishop and all the brother priests present. There is such a tremendous sense of commissioning from the People of God. It is patent within the ritual itself that the possibility of kindness helps the ordained to feel buoyed up, armored, supported, loved. The kiss of peace was a really beautiful experience for me, of being known and loved by parents and grandparents, siblings and aunts and uncles—and then somehow missioned by them for the Church. The imposition of the hands of the cardinal made me aware of how large the mission is, world-wide and centuries old. Those visceral moments seemed well orchestrated by a loving Church. I was grateful as could be to the masters of ceremonies, Peter Fink, SJ, and John Gallen, SJ, for all that they did to make it so. This gave me a lasting impression of how much I should do for anybody else who was receiving a sacrament through my work, as the hands of Jesus Christ. So, the ordination rite gives attention to the two edges of the sword of priesthood. Consider the triple elevation of the Liturgy of Ordination. It is a perfect image of what is offered by each of us in the Eucharistic Liturgy. First the bishop lifts the bread and wine as symbols of ourselves, our daily bread and wine that helps us to be friends in Christ. He lifts them separately; they represent both a kind of nononsense food and a free-flowing drink, nice symbols of both Aaron's and Melchizedek's priesthoods. He says the words, taken from ancient Hebrew worship: *Beruch ato Adonai*—"Blessed are You, Lord God, King of the universe, for You have given us this food and drink, fruit of the earth."

The second elevation of the bread and wine is at the consecration. Our gifts have been transformed by the work of the Holy Spirit into the Body and Blood of Christ. This "unbloody sacrifice" is again lifted separately. I believe that this makes dramatic, visceral, and imaginative sense of the fact that Jesus died, was killed, and His body and blood separated. This is a tender moment for me always in the Mass. I feel sometimes the gasping for His last breath as the veils of time and space are separated, like the Veil of the Temple, putting us right there in His eternal, divine moment, still on Calvary, still dripping His blood onto the rain-soaked earth, the ritual drama making sense to any who would pay attention. This is the moment of consecration pin-pointed in centuries of study.

Finally, at the end of the Canon, the Eucharistic Prayer, the bread and wine, now the Body and Blood are lifted together, symbolizing that the Christ we worship is also eternally and outside of our temporal dimension still divinely rising from the dead, Body and Blood reunited, Risen, true God and true Man. This is wondrous! A transfiguration! At every Eucharist Jesus, dead and risen, present, timeless, just moments apart for us. For those with eyes to see, for those with ears to hear…

The need to be aware of the sacred drama became very important to me right from the start. Whatever the priest can do to realize the reality beyond the time and space moment for himself, communicates itself to the congregation in some way. The realization leads to reverence in the priest; his reverence can encourage worship in the people. It seems simple enough. Just paying attention makes the reality more present in a human way. This is an ephemeral but most important responsibility of the priest, especially with the turning of the altar from the wall. The reverence of the priest becomes all-important to any member of the congregation who needs help attending to the sacred drama unfolding again in her/his midst. The problem, I think, exists for the priest in overcoming a certain understandable shyness about revealing this tender Faith in public. The priest is somewhat ashamed to be so naked before the ineffable Godhead, in front of all these strangers; this is, however, a great gift to bear for God, and for God's people. Ignatius of Loyola often spoke of "the gift of tears"; it is a humbling outpouring of which we should not be afraid. We need only ask the Holy Spirit for wisdom so we do not get in the way of Her grace. It is a fact that we claim the presence of the Holy Spirit in all of our sacraments. I have often had this understanding of the experience, which sometimes overwhelms me. It is shaking all over in a kind of pleasant spasm at the thought of the presence of God. Scotus referred similarly to a "shuddering" before the holy. I have come to think of it as the Holy Spirit within me recognizing and delighting in the physical or temporal presence of Jesus in the Eucharist. It's as though I am present in their reunion. I want to help others to shudder with the mysterious presence which will take their whole lives to comprehend. I do not want to get in the way of the Holy Spirit spreading Her wings over Her holy ones as She embraces our Lord within our own spiritual arms.

The best compliment I have gotten over the years has to be that I do not get in the way when I preside. It is a counterpart to what is probably the worst. The music minister thought that I was doing a serious wrong by using recorded popular music to show students just what I thought the readings were saying—in the words and rhythms of an idiom of their own present day. The music minister, as recounted earlier, said that I do bring a lot of people back to Church, but they are the wrong people and we don't want them. Sad commentary, yes, but a powerful rendering of the dangerous exclusiveness of or exclusion by the self-righteous.

12

Baptism

It was the time in this Mass of Baptism for lifting the unconsecrated elements. We call it the Offertory, the "minor elevation." The Roman Liturgy has for quite some decades made it clear to the congregation that these elements represent us humans, to whom have been given great gifts, at this time before the Consecration; we offer the bread and wine saying the ancient "berakah" prayer of the Hebrews, (*beruch ato Adonai....*)

> Blessed are You, Lord God, King of the Universe,
> For You have given us this bread to eat,
> Fruit of the earth and the work of human hands.
> Let it become our spiritual food.

Again, the bread at this point represents our working at being one body, because wheat is planted, harvested, crushed, kneaded, baked, and eaten—so many hands producing the "staff of life." While the wine is also the fruit of many laborers laboring, it represents the joy of fellowship, because this end product of comparable human work is not a necessity like bread, but something over and above. The sharing makes us more communal. Here at this baptismal liturgy, having just claimed the baby for Christ and called down the blessing of the Holy Spirit, it struck me that the Community should also offer the baby as a symbol of all of us—to be changed by the Holy Spirit through our commitment not only to God but to one another within the baptismal communion. So, I lifted the bread, said the prayer, lifted the cup, said the prayer, lifted the baby and said:

> Blessed are You, Lord God, King of the Universe,
> Wonder, Counselor, Prince of Peace,
>   and Everlasting Father,
> For You have given us this child to raise.
> May s/he be for us a sign of Your love and
> One day may s/he share the communion of this table.

It seemed so right that I have continued doing this. It is one of those personal expressions that a priest, with the advantage of all his training, is expected to share with his congregation. Every time that I have done this, the parents have felt overwhelmed and deeply awestruck at the enormity of what they have participated in. The wonder of human birth is put against the backdrop of the whole of God's creating. The rite of passage for the infant is thus a passage for the whole Church. Episcopalians carry the baby around the church, presenting the child, newly baptized, to the Church. This idea of presenting the child to God seems not far from that noble tradition, but it reinforces the idea that the baby is a gift from God to be given back after we and the Holy Spirit have worked our magic. It just seemed so right. I have big hands and am one of the oldest grandchildren of twenty-five on each side of my family. I am used to handling babies, holding them with their ears near my heart so they can hear it, and with their heads up so they can see all this interesting crowd. The unified families worship God as the maker of this particular miracle. It is natural for me to do something like this. But it became evident that this practice of mine has some universal primordial power. The parents are always moved, almost always to tears of awe at this moment in the Baptism. Sometimes the baby gazes at the father and wins his heart forever. It has been wondrous to me to observe that moment. I think of this as something that would be great for all baptisms of infants within the Christian communion, because it brings about a conversion of heart within the parents and families of the babies. Somehow in this moment, the awe-inspiring reality is almost too overwhelming to bear. God has given us this awesome gift. The Church is there to ask God's blessing and to remind us of the awesome responsibility to teach the child about grace, Jesus, the Virgin Mother, sacraments, etc. This is a way in which to preach without words. I am reminded, again, of the famous quotation of Francis of Assisi wherein he enjoins us to "preach always, sometimes use words." The awe-inspiring responsibility and honor of parenthood catches me off guard, and often my own eyes well with reverence before this mystery.

Another practice that I have learned to incorporate into Baptism is to pass the child's candle around the family. I try to find the elder within the family to be the first recipient of the taper lighted from the Paschal Candle. I remind the congregation that we all have learned of the Tradition because it was handed down to us, the Light of Faith, as a gift which we share, which we must share with one another and with the baby. This I learned from liturgy instruction with Ron Murphy, SJ, whose academic training in German Literature has made him especially sensitive to the power of symbolic action. Either in the greeting or in the homily we will already have had a consideration of the symbols associated with the sacrament. In the homily I usually light and blow out the paschal candle, saying that it represents our Faith in the Resurrection of Jesus. If there is a small child present, it is helpful to get him or her to help in naming the paschal candle or lighting the baby's candle and blowing out the flame and relighting it. I suggest that the lighting and blowing out of the paschal candle symbolizes our central belief in Jesus' resurrection. I also suggest that our faith goes out sometimes like a candle. I blow out the paschal candle and use the baby's candle to re-light it. "So, you see, little miracles shared by the members of the Church keep the Faith alive." These little hands, these little feet make it hard to deny that there is God. As this baby can rekindle awe and reinforce Faith, little acts of kindness can also rekindle a flickering faith; this is a miracle and a great wisdom of God's Church.

Having the children blow out the candles or say what color the white robes are keeps them interested but it also makes the family much more receptive. This is, for Jesuits, an old trick which St. Ignatius and his first companions used on mission; they engaged the children first and through them brought the parents around. This practice was quite instrumental in spreading the Gospel during the centuries of Spanish conquest and mission-building in the colonies. Whatever one thinks of the morality of spreading the seeds of the religion of one culture in the fields of another, the fact is that preaching to children helped spread the Good News of Christ to all corners of the world. This was, after all, one of Christ's last directives, "Go to all nations, baptizing them in the name of the Father, and of the Son, and of the Holy Ghost," remember?

Every sacrament is a sign which preaches all by itself—we have only to point out what the Church is saying in the rites. It also helps to remind the faithful that as adults we have probably had many doubts and that the small faith of one other member of the Church is often, through some act of kindness or wonder, enough to rekindle our own flame. A meaning of the baptism, then, for all the congregation, is that we depend on one another to rekindle our wavering Faith. The passing of the candle, which represents the new faith of the baby also then armors us, girds us with deeper faith and hope in the Church. The wonder we feel at considering the little fingers and the deep eyes of this bundle of possibility is a gift and a sign of the faith of the whole Church, built on graces, shared and treasured within the Body of Christ. This helps to found the belief of the parents, at least, in the "economy of salvation," the way in which the Church, sacramentally and communally, functions as the hands of God.

I enjoy talking about the white robe as a symbol of the armor that we receive sacramentally. Wearing an alb, like the elect around the throne of the Lamb in the *Book of Revelation*, I can reflect the light of the Paschal Candle. When they get that reference, I show the black clerical suit under the alb and say that we are all sinners in this Church but we can reflect the light of Christ, nonetheless, not by worth but by grace. Kids get this pretty well. I am comforted myself by admitting that I am a sinner and that the wonder of the sacraments depends on grace and not on my doing it right.

The final variation that I have found profoundly helpful occurs at the time of the blessing with oils. I first tell the people the difference between the Chrism by which the Church anoints the "neophyte" and the Oil of the Catechumens by which the congregation anoints their new member. It seems a natural distinction even though both oils are blessed by the bishop on Holy Thursday. This blessing of the oils, of course, links all three sacramental oils to the Eucharist which is celebrated on Holy Thursday as the commemoration of the "First Eucharist" when Jesus said the words at the Last Supper. However, the Oil of Catechumens is dispensed with all the hopes of the gathered community, this particular *ekklesia*, that the newly baptized will, indeed, be a worthy Christian.

Long after I have blessed the child at the beginning of the service with the chrism and claim him/her for Christ, I ask the congregation to bless the child after the baptism. Each individual, with the Oil of the Catechumens, then proceeds to the (usually) seated mother and says a prayer for the child. Thus, the Prayer of the Faithful for this particular baptismal liturgy is articulated as the hopes of the Church for every Christian child. It is the "Prayer of the Faithful" because it fits in right here after the baptism itself, after the readings and the Creed in question form, and before the Offertory. The particular hopes for this child are the universal hopes that we have for each member of the Ecclesia, that having become a Christian will make a difference in the way we live our lives. The expression of these hopes by the members of the congregation brings easy faith up from some. It also awakens some lethargic belief or hope or even love from an aunt or uncle who has been a stranger in Church. It calls them from the brink of un-faith, because of all the hopes placed on the child by the very people for whose love the uncle or aunt has come to church today.

The asking for these blessings, this Prayer of the Faithful contrasts with the blessing with water. The sign of the sacrament, the pouring of the water, is thus seen as the claiming of the blessing of the Holy Spirit; but the touch of the water itself is the action of God. The sacrament is the touch of the Spirit, seeming so ephemeral, but, to the eyes of Faith, so real. When we baptize the child, I invite all to touch the water to the baby and to bless themselves, recalling their own baptism. When I call down the blessing of the Spirit on the water, if there are any children present, I ask them to join me in asking for God's blessing, and I ask them to touch the water as I say the words of blessing. This reinforces the idea that God comes to us through our doing the ritual action that we see as having come from the Master Himself—the "sign instituted by Christ to give grace."

So these little tender explanations given during the administration of the sacrament become a way that a priest or deacon can help the Lord to say again, "Do you see what I have done for you?" The words from the Holy Thursday liturgy and the Last Supper narrative are the commentary on His own *diakonia*, His own serving by the washing of the feet. The work that a priest does to make the sacraments more tangible to the faithful is the work of helping us all to see what He has done for us. It is part of our calling. This preaching is subtle and easy because it simply helps the participant to *own* the ritual action and its consequences.

This kind of baptismal liturgy takes about an hour. I usually arrange for music, either real or recorded, because it adds so much. There are little processions for the baptism at the font itself, the anointing with the Oil of the Catechumens, going to the altar, and Communion. Music helps these little processions, but the choice can be crucial to the evangelization of the congregation!

It must be obvious by now that I am an academic-priest who is asked to baptize the children of family, students, and colleagues—friends. In other words, I seldom baptize, marry, or bury strangers. This is a privileged position. The priest in a large urban or suburban parish is often called on to preside over the rites of sacramental passage for complete strangers and often for many of them at once. This is a particular burden placed on them by the world in which we live. I know what that is like from a year or so in parish ministry during my early years as a priest. I know how hard it is to try to know people whom you have hardly met and yet to serve them where they really need God's healing hands. To be God's hands in an anonymous way like that takes a phenomenal spirit, listening deeply to the signs from God about His children right before us. This daunting endeavor, being a parish priest, should be a constant cause for great respect for those men who work for God's people in those demanding parochial roles.

My privileged position, as a "visiting priest," gives me a lot of leeway in presiding. I know and care about the people for whom I preside. This is a great advantage. I also have the leeway to linger, because typically there is no parking lot full of people waiting to fill the church for the next Mass. I am exempt from the barrage of complaints from controlling members of a local congregation who might always demand that the liturgy be conducted according to their lights. Free of those restraints, which often plague the parish priest, I can do things and study the responses with a great amount of academic distance.

It is this distance which allows me a greater experience (in the sense of larger or more diverse). I write these reflections to encourage my brother priests "in the trenches" to follow their hearts in dealing with God's people during the liturgies over which they preside. These suggestions I am making may be too cumbersome for some large parishes. On the other hand, some reflection will lead the generous priest to seek ways to preach without words more effectively. There is room for grace here. It is the kind of protection we used to call "the grace of office." In the office of presider, we stand for Jesus above all. He will come through us, if only we don't get in His way.

13

Marriage

The couple are the ministers of this sacrament, right? This is the teaching with which we have all been imbued at least since that articulation in the Baltimore Catechism, perhaps even longer. That has to mean more than something juridical, right? A powerful symbol is available as a statement of that reality during the nuptial liturgy. It comes when the priest, rather than asking another priest's blessing before he would presume to read the Gospel, asks the blessing of the couple before reading the gospel they've chosen for their marriage. It seemed a logical ritual, one that I, now, regularly ask the couple to consider, one which they are usually ready and willing to perform. It is a good time to remind all present that the priesthood of the People of God must be actualized by the Faith of the Church at work in the world. The sacrament of marriage is a Christ-identified model and focus of that work in the world.

For the priest this ritual can give a certain kind of fulfillment to the applause of the faithful at the ordination liturgy when the bishop said, in effect, "We rely on the testimony of the Church that these men are worthy to be ordained." The priest is also reminded of how his priesthood is for the people and that it needs the support of the people of God before it can be fruitful. This is a bonding moment between the priest and the couple, too. We remember how we have different graces, different gifts, and how we are interdependent in God's goodness.

Another thing that seems to work well at the wedding liturgy is for the couple to choose people to "set the table" as part of the Offertory. This helps to both distinguish and relate the two sacraments, the Marriage and the Eucharist. In this way, too, the couple can include more people in the celebration without needing to consider as an imposition how much those chosen would have to pay for attendants' clothing. Often, in my experience, siblings or grandparents have been chosen, but god-parents or best friends have also been the ones to set the table. This ritual can be accomplished simply by rolling up the two sides of the regular altar cloth and having it unfolded during the Offertory procession. It could also be more elaborate with a larger covering, depending on the style of the priest and the couple. But this ritual typically tells the whole congregation that the Mass is a Meal, the altar a table. I have often heard how evident it became, "as if for the first time," that, just as the table would be set by sisters or friends in the family home, the altar, the *mensa*-table, is set by them for this assembly. It really "strikes home," as it were. The groomsmen can then place the candles, the bridesmaids decorate the table with their bouquets and the reason for those roles becomes memorably clear. Those dear friends are chosen to help in the continuing ministry of the sacrament of marriage. Another benefit to the couple—no one in their wedding party feels like saying, "I paid such a great deal for these clothes to walk in and walk out of the church." They feel **involved** and somehow chosen. This is what I usually hear after such a ritual.

There is reluctance, I gather, to allowing the bride and groom to administer the Eucharist at their wedding. I have found, too, that some couples are reluctant to stand out in such a way. When the bride and groom do, however, stand beside me, holding the cups and saying the words, "the Blood of Christ," it seems to me that the *diakonia* aspect of their sacrament becomes much clearer to them, as well as to many of the congregation. If a sacrament means "a sign, instituted by Christ, to give grace," then the coming together of these two is as privileged in its way as is the priest's coming to the altar. This sacrament should be ratified at every possible moment so that the couple's participation in the High Priesthood of the Lord (see the *Epistle to the Hebrews*) will be supported by the Church and expected to bear fruit. This expectation itself will help to solidify the marriage in the spiritual life of the lay Church. I, for one, believe that this ministry should at least be exercised at the nuptial liturgy. Many brides and grooms take this encouragement and later become eucharistic ministers in their parishes after they have established themselves in an ecclesial community where they would bring up their family.

Of course, too, I encourage the couple to write their own Prayer of the Faithful, according to the norms set down in Joseph Champlin's wonderful *Together for Life* (Ave Maria Press 1970). He follows the dicta of the Roman ritual. I encourage the couple to actually read the Prayer of the Faithful. Most don't choose to do that but some do, and those seem to have a profound understanding that their marriage is not just for their happiness but has a priestly function in the life of the Church. They must somehow gather, collect, the prayers of the people and say them. This is a good example for us of how the family should function as a blessed community within the larger Church, with its own "elders" leading the community toward union with one another and with God.

Having the family of the groom stand in the aisle to pray over the ring of the bride before the priest blesses it, likewise for the bride's family to pray over the ring of the groom, is a poignant moment for the parents (no matter how many) and, often enough, even more so for the siblings. The joining of two families is made evident in the need for the family to pray for their new family member. "From now on this person who has married our brother, daughter, sister will be at Christmas dinner with us." It is good to have them pray together like this for him or her.

In the homily I say that it often must strike the congregation that an unmarried, childless priest is lecturing this young couple on the virtues and privileges of marriage. I try to get a laugh; usually at least, there is complete agreement from the entire congregation! Then I speak a little of Eugene Boylan's *This Tremendous Lover* (Newman Press 1948), wherein he says that the reality of the married is a type or image of the reality of the ordained and vowed men and women in the Church whose primary relationship is with God. This idea about the congruence of the struggles for authenticity in our love of God strikes home with so many of them. The realization that this sacrament must also be seen against the backdrop of each individual needing to grow in consciousness of God and in the ability to recognize God in their lives so that we will recognize God in death, is certainly sobering. The reality of it, though, is the reality that the Church must preach. All our dreams and hopes are like the beauty of the rose—destined for the dust. While the flower blooms, it should bless more than itself.

In the meantime we must make the best of it. The couple is intent on making the best of it through one another. It is good for the whole congregation to pray for both the couple and for the whole Church. This, too, is evangelizing without scolding.

Subtle gestures/profound statements

There are two other gestures that I have taken to incorporating into the ceremony which take the couple seriously as sacrament and as participants in the priesthood of Christ.

The first is during the *epiclesis*, that point in the Eucharistic Prayer when the priest calls down the blessing of the Holy Spirit on the gifts, before putting my hands over the bread and wine, but after beginning the prayer:

"Lord, You are holy indeed. Let Your Spirit come upon these gifts...to make them holy, so that they may become the body and blood of our Lord and Brother, Jesus Christ."

Right there where the pause comes, I let my hands hover over the heads of the Bride and Groom just before bringing them down to just over the gifts, where I make the sign of the cross. The idea is that calling down the blessing of the Holy Spirit is in the action of the hands; the wordless extension of the hands also over the heads of these two ministers of the Sacrament of Marriage asks the Holy Spirit to enter into this sacrament as well, making the couple into the Body and Blood of Christ. It is a wordless gesture, so making no profound theological statement literally, but a commanding prayer, a virtual claim, just the same.

The other gesture comes at the Our Father. This one is more evident to the couple than to the congregation. I often preface it by telling the congregation the meaning of the gesture. I wrap the joined hands of the couple in my stole, praying that the Church will be there for them when they need her, that they will become part of the ministry of the Church for others. It is quite obvious and a very visceral drama. The couple as well as the congregation gets the point. Again, I think of this as preaching without words, an added meaningful gesture which any presider could incorporate into the ceremony.

So these simple gestures, adding so much, actually take the teaching of the *magisterium* at its word and put an action on the theology. The additions are not without precedent; they speak volumes, but they are not presently written into any ritual book. Are they taking too free a look at the ritual? I don't think so. They are so simple and so subtle that they can be missed, like so much of the ancient ritual, if we do it without paying attention. Again, "for those who have ears to hear, let them hear; for those with eyes to see, let them see."

14

Wedding Letter

The wedding preparation itself can be such a graced time. I find myself asking the questions about in-laws, sexual prerogatives, money management, the number and timing of children, and the desire to pray every day together at the same time and in the same place. To be sure, since I am asked to preside at weddings by people who know me, as teacher, family member, or friend, I have a privileged experience, quite different from what it was like when I worked in a parish. However, I still think that it is important to ask the hard questions, because the couple allows me to say things and ask things that their closest friends and family, oftentimes, can't easily address. I tell myself that I may ruin the relationship that I am building with these two, but that service to the Church demands that *someone* ask what needs to be asked. I also recommend that the couple do the diocesan program of Pre-Cana or Engaged Encounter; it seems to me that more rather than less preparation for this sacrament is what these two should get from asking a friend to preside. It's also a great way to emphasize that their sacrament is a sacrament of and for the larger Church.

All of that having been said, the wedding itself is a wonderful "teaching moment." The couple and their families and friends can learn so much about sacramental meaning in their lives through the preparation for the ceremony itself. I always prefer to run the rehearsal and I let it take as long as it takes (typically more than an hour). This practice has won me many scowls from clergymen in the parishes where I am a guest presider at the wedding. I often hear: "If these people get this kind of treatment everybody else will expect it."

Too often have I been told that the reason I take so long with rehearsal is that I don't know what I am doing. These guys hit where they think educators are most vulnerable! But, if they actually stayed for the rehearsal, they'd see that there are many "teaching moments" in a rehearsal. I must admit to feeling a little guilty at seeming to place a clerical colleague on the defensive in his own bailiwick, but I figure he will get over it. It does cause me some wonder that someone would get so put out by my taking more time at a rehearsal than he would; after all, he is completely relieved of the responsibility. Maybe there's the rub; somehow the local priest might feel implicitly rejected by the couple's choosing an "outsider" to do the service. For this I can feel sorry, but an apology would be inappropriate. Dealing with another's feelings is such a tricky business; it is important to keep the Lord's compassionate example in mind. Besides, I don't ever really know *why* they asked me, so I can't explain to my unknown colleague, my inner drive to "professional courtesy" notwithstanding.

It has become, therefore, my practice to be as grateful and as gracious as I can be to the hosts in the parish. Priests and wedding coordinators deserve the respect I expect them to give me, too. I recommend that the couple realize that we are beholden to the local staff even if they pay for the privilege. This, too, is an opportunity for them to learn for the future that the parochial staff are professionals and brethren within the community—not people who merely serve and can therefore be treated as servants. This is a delicate series of interactions. Make no mistake about it.

The letter which follows is one which I commonly send to prospective couples, even if they are family or very close friends. It helps to remind them of their prerogatives and responsibilities as well as to teach them about the meaning of ritual action. The result can be a greater openness to and more awareness of the richness of all the Church's rituals. The letter obviously creates an opportunity for the priest to work with the couple. Again, I think this is a privilege which we should cherish, even though it is a great taxation on our time and energy. We will not be paid for all the work (certainly nowhere near as much as the DJ or the caterer!) but it will be appreciated.

The letter

Thank you so much for asking me to take part in your wedding. It is a tremendous honor! This letter is a copy of one that I sent to my cousins twenty-five years ago. It has lots of things for you to think about and discuss. Then we can talk, OK? It is a great privilege both to represent the People of God and to be so close to your preparation for receiving and perpetuating the sacrament who is always the Lord.

Now about the wedding itself! There are so many things to think about and to pray about but, if we look at them in some logical sequence, it will not seem confusing and you'll know just what you have to think and pray about.

First, let's establish the order of the normal Mass, the eucharistic liturgy, which is adapted for the wedding.

These are the parts:

▶ Entrance*
▶ Greeting prayer, penance rite, Kyrie*
▶ Readings (O.T., song, N.T., [song,] Gospel)
▶ Homily*
▶ Creed [We don't usually do this at weddings]

▶ Prayer of the Faithful ———

▶ Offertory (setting the table)*

▶ Canon (Preface, Sanctus, Consecration, Acclamation Prayer, Amen)

▶ Our Father ———

▶ Kiss of Peace*

▶ Agnus Dei (Lamb of God), breaking of bread ———

▶ Communion

▶ Benediction*

▶ Exit

   * The kiss-of-peace is mentioned where it usually shows up, but the asterisks are placed where it may be moved if it would make more sense given the theme or needs of the particular liturgy.

There are also little "lines of possibility," those dashes after the Our Father for instance (———), throughout the Mass, where other things might occur. Of particular interest for us is the placing of the exchange of vows, though there are also other possibilities—rings, candles, flowers, flowers at the altar of the Mother of God, incense, etc.

Now there are many options for you to consider in light of this order of the Mass:

FOR THE ENTRANCE

Do you want to enter the Church in the traditional way, i.e., the Bride preceded by her "ladies in waiting" coming to the altar rail, where all are met by the Groom and the groom's men, including the priest. Is there a rail? Remember that each and every movement of the ritual-action of the People of God has meaning. The meaning either speaks for itself or it needs a little explanation. The things that you two do at your wedding are, somehow, taken out of the realm of the everyday; they are no

longer "profane," but sacred. They become no longer "prescribed," but your own. What you do is prayer, and each thing
you do, before God and His people—your people—is a statement of the meaning of marriage, Church, prayer, love, commitment, family, God, Faith, or any of the things held sacred by
the people you have gathered to share this precious moment
when you *sacramentalize* your love for each other. So, back to the
point, do you want this traditional movement or some other?

POSSIBILITIES

The groom, presented by his parents, comes down the aisle
before the bride, presented by hers or by the ladies-in-waiting,
the groom presented by all the men (including, perhaps, the fathers of both)—the bride by all the ladies (including, again perhaps, the mothers), etc., etc., etc. In other words, decide on
the *statement* of the entrance, what you want it to say about
where you are each coming from.

How do you want to occupy the sanctuary? Kneeling with
backs to the congregation is an old tradition (as from the movies
about the coronation of kings), but it has this problem: the bride
and groom have not the ability to watch and welcome the guests,
or the ability to preside at the assembly, the *ecclesia*. Besides, they
have their backs to "the audience" and this, for many, feels un-
comfortable. For others, it is exactly right. You might choose to
sit facing the people during the readings and the opening re-
marks (including the homily). For this the "shape" of the sitting
means something—women on one side with the bride, men on
the other, with the priest in the middle? Another option, men
and women interspersed with the priest to one side? Another
option: bridesmaids and groomsmen in the first pew? There are
other options, depending on the physical setup of the particular
sanctuary.

READINGS

Who's doing the readings? What are the readings? Do the readers come into the sanctuary before the bridal party? Do they come just at the time of their readings? Do they have a place to sit in the sanctuary? Are they to be accompanied by the priest? Or by the groom? Or an acolyte? Do they read from the same pulpit? Or from the altar rail? Or from their places in the congregation? Do the bride and groom intend to introduce the readings with reasons for the choice of readings or readers? Do the bride and/or groom want to do a reading? Are you printing the readings in a booklet? This last is a good way to remember ten, fifteen, fifty years down the road!

HOMILY

Who will do the homily? Shall I or another?

PRAYER OF THE FAITHFUL

Who will do the prayer of the faithful? Will it be spontaneous? Will the congregation be invited to prayer? Will the bridal party be asked to say something prepared? Something unprepared? Will the bride and/or groom say prayers for the congregation, this, their chosen Church? You two really ought to write your own prayers for the wedding day and then you or someone else can read them, leading the congregation in prayer (with them saying or singing: "Lord, hear our prayer" or some other such formulaic response).

THE MEAL-EUCHARIST

It's a good idea to separate the meal-Eucharist from the vow-ritual, making the meal seem so normal that all know this is family. Setting the table and placing the gifts on it is very much what will happen in your home. This first meal where the Lord is both meal and chef is where you will first host your guests at a banquet as husband and wife. This is a profound moment in your lives together. How will the table be set? Who will set it— bride and groom, best-man and maid-of-honor, parents of the bride and groom, chosen guests? Will there be an offertory procession? Will a chosen guest be asked to bake the bread, to make or buy the wine, to supply a bread basket, to make a chalice or buy one (ceramic, silver, crystal, wood, china, other)? Will a separate cover be used (large table cloth, small one)? Will the flowers be set on the altar at this time? Will there be candles? Will your parents light them? Will you later use these candles to light one representing Christ in your marriage? (The paschal candle could be used to represent Christ entering into this sacrament instead of a commercial unity candle.) Do you want to save the candles? Remember that this is the first time that you two will be having guests at your banquet as man and wife. The Lord will be present; it will be special. What will be most meaningful to you?

STANDING BEHIND THE ALTAR

Do you want to stand with the priest behind the altar for the Canon (the Eucharistic Prayer)? Do you want the bridal party there? Parents? Brothers? Sisters? The whole congregation standing in the sanctuary? (Is it big enough?)

KISS OF PEACE

The Kiss of Peace is the response to the recommendation from the Lord, Jesus, the Christ, Himself, that we not come to the altar of sacrifice without making peace with our brothers and sisters first. Does the kiss of peace belong here or elsewhere before communion in your Wedding Mass? Does it belong earlier? At the very beginning? As part of the Penance Rite? Is there a special need to deal with reconciliation?

THE VOWS

Do the vows belong before Communion or before the Offertory (the "regular" place)? At the altar? In the space before the altar? In the aisle with the people? Do you want the parents to be closer to the rite of the vows itself? Should the vows be, perhaps, before the Canon altogether, as part of the Offertory Rite, meaning, implied by the placing of the vow ceremony, making your marriage an offering. Will you be husband and wife before the Canon, at the Offering, at the Kiss of Peace, or at the reception of the Lord's Body and Blood? Will you make up your own vow formula?

For the vow formula in the Roman Catholic Church, there are two very important principles which must be included, *until death* and *come hell, high water, or happiness* ("in sickness or in health, in good times and bad, for richer for poorer, until death do us part"). It seems to me that your vows are the most important part of the ceremony for each of you.

You vow before God and His people, your chosen Church, to stay together and work to find Him in your relationship. It is awesome! Pray apart and together, then write apart and then together the things you would vow to each other. Make a formula which says the things it should say in your own prayerful words. During the ceremony itself, the words thus written on your hearts will be the ones heard by God and by each of you, no matter what words come out of your mouths, your own formula or one of the ones in the book.

BLESSING THE RINGS

Lately, I have found that asking the family of the bride and groom to pray over and bless the rings has been a wonderful thing. The family, knowing the bride or the groom best, prays for the other one, asking God to give her/him whatever s/he needs to live with their son/ brother/ daughter/ sister. The family also prays to enfold the new member into the fabric of their own family.

COMMUNION

How will we do Communion? One option is for the priest to give the Body of Christ and the bride and groom to give the two cups of His Blood. You may have other ideas. Are there Eucharistic ministers present?

OTHER POSSIBILITIES

Are there any other things you want to do? Pray at the altar for children, healthy and godly? Blow out two candles and light one? Place flowers on Mary's altar? Give gifts to your parents? Say some words of thanks or sharing?

BLESSING

Do you want everyone to raise hands and call down the Holy Spirit?

LEAVING

Any special ideas about the leaving?

Well, I suppose this looks like a real lot of stuff to think about and to discuss, pray over, and decide. Call (after 11:00 pm 'till 2:00 am is fine) when you have some ideas and some questions. I'll try to help as much as I can. It honestly seems to me a graced moment in two lives, a marriage. This is the time to question all sorts of things about yourselves and about your relationships—to God, to others and to the institution/community (Church). That's what I take as motivation for asking all sorts of questions; I like to spend a few hours of preparation with a couple asking all kinds of things about falling in love with others, about children, about money, about housework—figuring that it's an opportunity that I have, uniquely; they needn't like me for my own sake and that gives me a freedom that few in their lives have. At any rate, these questions usually get asked while discussing the meaningful ritual actions of the wedding day. The answers come with decisions about why the bride or groom wants to do this or that. A lot of education usually occurs during the discussions.

You two are certainly able to get all of that out of this discussion on your own—if you ask God to grace your talk. The outcome of all this will be, with God's grace, your own ceremony wherein the ritual speaks to you, for you. The rehearsal should normally take less than two hours, the wedding just over one.

Why should we plan so long for the rehearsal? Well, remember you two are the ministers of the Sacrament of Marriage, I the minister of the Eucharist. The coordination must belong to all those that you've asked to be part of it; they must know their parts and why their parts are what they are. The rehearsal is also my time, as "director"; this is when I get down just what you want so that on the day itself I know what to do and how to direct everyone through your ceremony—so that you two can relax and completely enjoy your work on that glorious day.

I hope all this seems clear and good. Let's pray that the Lord, God the Father, in Jesus' Name, send the Holy Spirit to us in this glorious work of thanks and praise.

One final thing! On the day itself, after you will have done all this work, your hearts will already be married. The day is a celebration of that, but the sacrament is the asking and receiving of the Lord's presence, the grace of the Holy Spirit. This is a perduring blessing promised through the ministry of the

Church and prayed for by these people who love you. Don't miss the day! Rely on your friends to carry out the great preparations. You try to hold on to the moments; take mental snapshots, write mental notes, remember—remember. Then, when people show you pictures, you'll be able to enjoy your own memories (rather than having to invent them out of other people's memories). So on the day itself, do what you can to be totally relaxed and to trust God to do the blessing. OK?

Thanks again for honoring me with taking part. It is a tremendous privilege.

Final thoughts

So that's the letter. There is a lot for the couple to think about. They cannot handle all the thoughts, of course, at such a time. But they do have a sense of this being their wedding, their Church, and that there is some hard work that goes into making it be God's Church, smooth running, accessible, and beautiful. If there are decisions still to be made by the time of the rehearsal, I do my best to get the couple to make them. In fact, I say that we will do the rehearsal twice; the first time anybody may ask questions or make suggestions and the bride and groom will decide. The second time through is for me to get the stage directions right; this time through is wordless and should take no more than three to five minutes. It works. The wedding is the most taxing of all the sacraments for which I prepare people. I do believe that the work is worth it. I do this between ten and twenty times a year and still feel that this is God's work and we are blessed in it. Perhaps, if I had to witness two weddings a week, I would be less enthusiastic. But if I were to organize a team who would help the couples in my parish to prepare for marriage, I would hope that they would engage in such preparation with gusto and grace.

Of course, at present in many dioceses the rules are becoming quite stringent. There is a move to *regularize* the nuptial liturgy so that no one thinks of themselves as special, because we all belong to God's Church. I hope that a sense of the integrity of individual gifts will return to the practice of sacramentalizing the marriage of particular people in God's name and in God's Church, according to the gifts that God has already given to these particular people and in the hope that their gifts, through their sacrament and with an increase of charity through its graces, will become more and more integrated into the faith life of the larger Church.

15

Sacrament of the Sick

In my experience, although Marriage is the most taxing sacramental preparation, the Sacrament of the Sick is the most difficult of sacraments to be prepared for. This is so because the person who needs the sacrament can be found in almost any state from conscious to comatose, in great pain or at great peace. The priest may be called for the "Last Rites" or he may be asked to pray over someone who has not yet had a surgical procedure. The possibilities are endless. The preparation is long-term and general, the execution: "fly by night," the rite quite simple or elaborate, accordingly.

The "accordingly" part is mostly up to the priest and his take on the situation. The call to be priest according to the order of Melchizedek is really clear—and taxing—in this situation, because a particular person is in great need of kindness, needing food for the mind, perhaps, and drink for the spirit. That much is clear. The proximity of death can render the most controlling of us somewhat awestruck and pliant.

However, sometimes the family and friends in attendance are expecting the priest, through the ministry of the Church, to perform a miracle. The kind they want is not usually one of the viable options. But there is the miracle of Christ. We come to bring Him and the healing that the Holy Spirit is willing to impart. It seems to me that the most important thing we can do is to help both the sick person and those in attendance to be attentive to the loving presence of God. Readings may be taken from the *Pastoral Care of the Sick* ritual book, the sacramentary, the bible, or some text pertinent to the sick person and his/her entourage. There could be singing or recorded music. Confession might be heard. Conditional absolution may be administered if the sick person is unconscious or mentally or virtually absent. The Oil of the Sick may be placed on the body of the sick person, and Communion, *viaticum*, may be taken. All of these things can take a long time or a short time. Again, according to the priest's reading of the situation.

Saint Ignatius' principle of the *"magis,"* the more, comes into play here. What procedure would be more conducive to helping the sick person be at peace with God and the world s/he may soon leave? This is what we should try to facilitate.

The important thing, moreover, is to be kind and solicitous. It is also useful for the priest to put on the stole at the moment he wishes to turn from visiting to presiding at ritual. Putting on the stole sacramentalizes the whole room and people calm themselves and allow us to preside. This is a clear indication of the power of the cultic priest, the levitical priest, according to the *Order of Aaron*; the people allow us to take over at this most difficult time. It is a privilege, yes, but a major and somewhat terrifying responsibility, because we should help them all to pray without our getting in the way. The easiest way to avoid knowing whether or not we are in the way would be to just say the prayers, anoint the patient, and get out of there. The opportunity to do a more real service, helping the sick to relax and to accept God's healing, or to help the dying to relax and accept the final coming, might be diminished by our hasty retreat. Remember, we seek to do the *"magis,"* what is more conducive to God's greater glory. There are lots of good things to do; we look to do the best that we can do, in respect to God's glory.

The opportunity to do great good for the dying, moreover, is surpassed by the seemingly greater good that can be done for those remaining. The family and friends of both the sick and the dying can be armed with grace by our courage in the face of a difficult emotional situation to be courageous themselves. The example of undaunted Faith can be a great help to those who are worried and grieving. A little time, a little effort does involve us, but not forever. People, no matter how needy at such a moment, have their own lives to live. Most often, the lesson learned is taught by the teacher and forgotten. In truth, though, the unforgettable Teacher is the Messiah; the Father is God, who will never forget! Remember that Jesus, in *Matthew*, says, "call no one 'father'... no one 'teacher' ... except the One." So our little involvement will probably not become an entangling alliance; our irenic moment of serene hieratic benediction will allow the Lord to enter.

I have found it good to have enough eucharistic hosts, if I am bringing Viaticum, to offer it to those in attendance. I also find it good to offer the Oil to them so that they might touch the sick with God's promise through this ministry of the Church. Their healing happens in the touch, too. But more importantly, I want to afford the Holy Spirit more opportunity to work wonders.

Once, when the patient was a tragic burn victim, unable to speak and looking quite as if the end was near, although, miraculously, it was not, I risked something. I told the three teen-aged children that, if they loved her, they should tell their mother. I really don't know if that was a risk well taken. The young people were apparently in a trance and seemed unable to quite fathom what I was saying, but they each told her that they loved her, touching her on a place that was not burned. She could not see them or speak, but she yelled loudly from somewhere deep within. She did live. I still have no idea, humanly, if that was the right thing to suggest. But I did pray for Wisdom and tried to pay attention to the "still small voice" of God within. I do this often and pray for the courage to risk following my gut, which is tantamount to giving my responses over to God as His tools.

This way I try to be, and trust that I am, His instrument. For me, this is really trusting that God will use the little things of this earth to accomplish His wonders. Little can be said about this powerful ministry—the sacrament can be administered by anyone, almost. The minimal sacrament is wondrous in its maximal potential, so clear the way; God works through the willing servant.

Another personal example

Once, I was called at 3:00 AM. Security at our university had put the call through to me. A student at another university in town was stabbed that afternoon. He'd been a quarterback at a football game, returned to his room hungry, asked his friends if anyone wanted to accompany him to a local fast-food chicken place. There were no takers, so he went alone; it was very early for dinner but he was famished. A crazed person came into the chicken place and stabbed a number of people. This young man was stabbed a number of times, twice in the heart.

His roommate had promised the boy's parents that he would get a priest. The priests from the two Catholic parishes which serve the hospital chaplaincies said they would come to the hospital if the boy died. After many hours of surgery and mounting worry, with a very large contingent of students gathering at the hospital, this roommate had gotten me. He was quite insistent that he wanted me to come down to the hospital. I live in a dormitory and couldn't find it in my heart to refuse. Driving down there close to 3:30 AM, I told the Lord that I didn't know any of these kids, I was nervous about what was expected and more about what I could do. I told Him I was doing this as though the boy were Himself.

At the hospital ER doors, there were a few police cars. A hospital guard met me and said, beaming, "I knew the Catholics would come through." I got to a waiting room with fifty students asleep on the floor. A lovely young man in a light blue clerical shirt greeted me. He was the Presbyterian chaplain; he told me apologetically that the students would only settle for a Catholic, because the victim was Catholic. The fellow who'd called me was no longer on the premises. A few of the kids got up and begged me to go into the OR. The chaplain said that was impossible. I thanked God for his presence, his kindness, and his forthright wisdom. I asked if there were a chapel or someplace to pray. There was, right across the hall. I would go there and pray.

The room was quite large, mystically quiet, comforting, but very formal. I told the young sleepy crowd, who'd all gotten up to pray with me, that I would say a couple of prayers, wait for their prayers and end with an Our Father. They prayed tentatively, I thought, but nothing was said other than the words I spoke.

While we were saying the Our Father, a nurse came in, whispered to the Presbyterian minister and left. As we said, "Amen," he asked, "Did any of you hear what she just said? Your friend has survived surgery, is in recovery (after eight or nine hours on the table) and it looks like he's going to be all right."

I swear I felt like a bow in the hands of a sacred violinist like Itzak Perlman, Isaac Stern, or Jascha Heifitz. God is good. The young man called me ten months later to report that he was back in school, just to thank me for showing up when he needed me. All that and a Thank You, too! But the "sacrament of the sick"? I certainly didn't get to do anything with the Oil or the Eucharist. But the sacrament? I think God did use a sign to give grace.

16

Funeral

The greeting of the mourners at the front of the church is an important step in putting the grieving at ease. The thought of these "last rites," the ritual of sending the beloved home to God, is very sad for those saying good-bye, but they seem comforted by being encouraged to consider that, though they are sad, their beloved is on the verge of the beatific vision. Before starting the commemoration of baptism, it has become my practice to tell the family at the door what this ritual is really about; it is to admit our own grief, but even more, in view of our FAITH rather than our knowledge, we are celebrating the liberation of our beloved. Poetically true, the speaking of it in church helps the bereaved feel not alone. The sharing of this hope, in the presence of the living loved ones, can build HOPE. It emphasizes our dependence on the LOVE and promises of Christ.

After the greeting and having the pall-bearers or the immediate family place the pall on the coffin, I remind the congregation that the cloth reminds us of the white cloth of baptism. I use more words than simply reading the opening in the ritual book. We are claiming for the dead the promise of baptism. Baptism called for the abiding presence of the Holy Spirit and promised the prayer of the Church;

these are what we claim for the dead. As Church, we claim both the promise of the People of God and the hope we have that God will be true. As Elizabeth said of Mary, "You believed that God would be true to His promises" (*Luke* 2); we claim this belief for ourselves. It does not remove intellectual doubt, but it reinforces sacramental Faith. Practically, speaking in plain words rather than immediately in ritual voice prepares the congregation to accept the ritual; at the portal it eases the passage from *profane* to *sacred* space.

Later, I explain the "meaning" of the cloud of smoke released in the incensing. The two-fold meaning is balm to the mourners. On the one hand, we are recalling the Presence of God as betokened in the desert when Yahweh said to Moses that He would be with them as a pillar of fire by night and a column of cloud by day. On the other hand, our prayers ascend as does this smoke, lifting our beloved to God. Both explanations make a somewhat arcane ritual make eminent sense, sensual sense, to the congregation. As with any good ritual, it makes the reality go deeper. Understanding the symbol makes the ritual itself go deeper. Even for the well-informed, small bits of ritual have little meaning unless they are brought into sharp focus. At a time of grief, simple reminders of what the actions mean are grasped where deeper thoughts are hard to bear. I learned of the need and the power of the explanation from Sr. Caritas McCarthy, SHCJ, from Rosemont College, a double-doctorate professor of history, who understood the need, even among academics, for an explanation of "the obvious" in ritual, at sensitive moments. This is one of the jobs of the priest, is it not, to preach always? Again, as St. Francis of Assisi put it, "Preach always; when necessary, use words." I believe that when people are caught up in emotion, the words that they are given to focus on the present help the ritual do its job better. So sometimes use words.

I find that making some veneration of the coffin or the "cremains" (hateful word!) is a good thing, respectful of the deceased and meaningful to the bereaved. If it would have been appropriate to kiss or touch the arm of the dead person when s/he was alive, it would be most appropriate to reverently touch or kiss the coffin. It can't be forced; that would come across as false intimacy. It counters a dictum of many liturgists of our day, namely, "Kiss nothing that can't kiss you back!" but it seems so real, so sensuous, so appropriate to reverence some things this way. It speaks to the bereaved. I believe it somehow speaks to them of Jesus.

The end of the Mass of Christian Burial is the time when eulogies are delivered. Some families have great need for lots of words. Most do not. I believe that allowing more people to take up our time at the end of the Mass is usually a profound kindness, taking the place of the wake, which has become all too often a waste of time in our culture. Like those who "sit *shivah*" for the deceased of the Chosen People, we are there to comfort the living, as all those who come to the funeral are there to comfort the living. The time spent by the priest might seem, because of the sense he has of doing his job, to be wasted, just sitting there an intolerably long time. But I figure, I have just made them listen to me; this is a little of my own medicine. I should "take it like a man." Attention to the congregation will tell the attentive presider if it is time to call an end to it. We must remember that those outside our profession are less acquainted with death than we. It is a kindness to wait for them to finish—or not. The difference is important to broker the time in a way that speaks not of annoyance but of accommodation is our responsibility.

Standing at the door while the congregation files past is also a courtesy well worth the time spent. We act as host for the Lord, Who is now the new Acquaintance of the deceased and Who has just thanked the friends and family for the new arrival in His promised land. It is a thing that we, in His name, should do—stand at the door thanking the mourners in the name of God's greater Church. It is especially good to be gracious to those who seldom see the inside of a church; it can encourage them to "come home." Remember the very meaning of "Eucharist" is literally "well-blessed"; the word is still modern Demotic Greek for "thank you." We can continue thanking in God's name and in the name of the deceased.

At the cemetery, I find that music is comforting, more so than spoken words. So I do some prayer and reading from the ritual book, but also have a CD or two that might bookend the service at the tomb. Music, while the family and friends place flowers on the coffin, is a good way to end. There is some uplift to the closure. Funeral directors often comment on how much better it seems with music, not so cold and relentless—"I'm going to keep a CD player in the hearse, Father, for when I have to do the service myself."

The idea of flowers containing seeds is easily put into parallel with the words of the Lord about the grain of wheat falling into the ground and dying before it can become new life. Recall briefly for them that the dead person's life is now planted in the hearts of the grieving. If the love is cherished and the living do good in the name of the deceased, the seed shall have taken root and will blossom in the lives of those standing at the grave. It is good to remember that loving carries responsibilities well beyond the seeming termination of this place. This kind of reflection is very easily understood by children; actually addressing children at the grave makes the adults more attentive. This also focuses, without saying it, on life perduring—"Life goes on." We owe it to the dead to take care of the living.

It must be obvious by now that I believe all the sacraments are signs which speak powerfully to us of God's love, even more when we attend to the congregation's needs, from our role as Christ's representative. One problem for us, in today's technologically connected world, is that we have come to pass by truths with little notice. Television and the Internet have made global events immediately knowable to us. We have also taken to considering that the media interpret the facts before they report them. There is often a keen sense of disbelief whenever facts are being reported.

For us in the business of prayer, the "facts" are the eternal ones. It is the response to eternal truths that resulted in the writing of Sacred Scripture. It is the response to the eternal Truth of Jesus' life that resulted in the historical development of the sacraments. In the "new evangelism," called for by John Paul II in recent years, the priest's own history plays an important part in his preaching. It is my contention that our preaching about the very things we do in the rites is telling the story at its center. This is how in Benedict XVI's masterful understanding, we bridge the gap between *eros* and *agape*. We use the filial (or *philial*) relationships and the power of erotic love to help the congregation to commune with the living, the suffering, and the dead, to come out of themselves and to take care of one another. We encourage them to *caritas*. "God is Love," after all! (1 *John* 4)

To help the people understand the scriptures, we labor over the readings, meditating, doing both primary and secondary research, bringing in events of the day or of our own lives. We do our best to make the scriptures come alive.

It is also our duty to make the rituals come alive. It is amazing to me how many adults, committed Catholics, have never been to the Good Friday Liturgy. How few people have ever thought about why we use incense at a funeral? What is the meaning of the paschal candle? The rites are so rich. There is so much to gain by information. This is part of our job, both as Aaronic priest—helping the people to perform appropriately the rites of passage through the rituals of the Church and, as priest in the order of Melchizedek—helping the people to see that God loves us, beyond all comprehension, constantly giving according to our need, helping them to see what the rites imply in the people's response, namely that we must love as God commands.

My own experience? Again, all these thoughts have arisen after years of burying beloved dead. Sixty people in my family have died since I became conscious of the Other and the Other's world. I have buried forty-seven of them, many of them quite young. My realizations about what works arise from a very involved attention to my familial congregation. Not all of my family appreciates the things that I do, but most recognize that it comes from an educated heart;

some are able to tell me how much it meant to them that I said or did something. The reality is, of course, that any coming out of self is a risk. I leave myself open to criticism. But if I don't do what I think I must for these people here and now, well then, who will?—and when? I can only do my best and trust God to give the Wisdom. Further, what I would do for my family in the flesh, I must try to do for my family in the spirit. What I have learned from understanding my family's grief and my own empowers my ability to care for the families and friends of strangers in God's family.

17

Eucharist

In my study of architectural and liturgical history over the years before and since my dissertation, which resulted in the two books mentioned above, I have found many surprising things that make for good discussion about the origin and meaning of some of our more unquestioned Eucharistic traditions. Let's consider a couple of them.

We do not actually know very much about the earliest liturgical era just after the Resurrection. Jungmann says that there were meetings in homes and larger places. Eventually, after the fourth century Edict of Milan, when the Church became acceptable within the Empire, there were large basilicas built specifically for the Christian assembly, like Constantine's Basilica of St. Peter in Rome and his and Justinian's later reconstruction of Hagia Sophia in Constantinople. In a couple of centuries there was a vast growth of the community, and the liturgy became more uniform in certain centers. Different liturgies developed in cultural *milieux,* with political overtones and princely artistic preferences prevailing. The East Syrian Rite, the West Syrian Rite, the Mozarabic, the Antiochene, etc, and later the Milanese, the Gallican Rites, and the Latin Rite grew from many roots to the development in the West of what was finally regularized as a single tree, into what became, after the Council of Trent, the "Tridentine Rite" of the Missal of Pius V.

Many good things from our past have shadow sides, even unto the present. Like the Holocaust which should never be forgotten, the Crusaders' attacks on the Eastern Churches should be systematically recalled. The fight over the *filioque* phrase, by which we acknowledge, in the Nicene Creed, that the Holy Spirit *proceeds* from both the Father **and the Son**, is, after all, the acknowledged proximate cause of the Great Schism, whereby the Eastern Orthodoxies became separated from the Western Patriarchate. This is a terrible event in the history of Christendom, but we celebrate it every week in the Sunday liturgy. I cannot say those words without remembering that this is as sad a part of our history as were some of the regrettable historical moments in the Renaissance/Reformation. There is much to regret in the Spanish Inquisition, as it hovered over so much of Christendom with a "holy terror." The Enlightenment followed close on the heels of the "Counter Reformation," leading to great destruction of holy places and murderous attacks on cultural centers of religion in a "Reign of Terror." This is the kind of truth that I would personally like to expand as we remember *"illud tempus,"* Eliade's immortal phrase commemorating that time when God was with us, by returning to Greek, Latin, and Hebrew refrains: God has not rejected us for any of our major gaffs in reading His will for us. We need to acknowledge and to celebrate Their constant Trinitarian tenderness. They have come with us through all these vicissitudes of time and politics. They are still with us.

I, for one, would prefer to see our roots reflected better in the liturgy that we celebrate universally. For instance, I really like the triple *Kyrie eleison, Christe eleison, Kyrie eleison* which had, at least since the Sixth Century development of Gregorian Chant, been sung with lovely tunes and then extremely intricate and beautiful harmonies (Palestrina, Gabrielli, and Allegri, et al), and later still with tremendous musical accompaniment (Bach, Beethoven, Mozart, Haydn, Handel) and more recently with more romantic flare (Fauré,

Franck). Rachmaninoff and Tchaikovsky have done *Kyries* for Eastern Rite liturgies that have been adopted by the West. More recently still are the stunning Rutter, Bernstein, and Lloyd Weber works. Paul Winter's *Missa Gaia* and Ariel Ramirez' *Missa Criolla* bring modern rhythms to the ancient form. Many more accessible musical traditions now abound, but in the vernacular they lose that ancient connection. So the *Kyrie*, in the Greek of the Early Church, reflecting our most ancient traditions with an Hebraic proclivity for a triple, triple rendition of the prayer has a very long and continuous history throughout the first two millennia of the Church's existence. It is sad that we have cut off that bi-millennial tradition for the sake of the vernacular, with our persistent penchant for austere logicality. The faithful are quite capable of comprehending that we have roots in other languages, willing even to say or sing them. The continuity with the past is powerful.

There was need, of course, to follow the lead of the Holy Spirit at the time of the Vatican Council reforms. It was thought that the whole Tridentine tradition had to be sacrificed, or modulated, I suppose, so that its stranglehold on the living, breathing, liturgical life of the Church could be broken. Now that there have been so many reforms, wouldn't it be wise to reclaim the best of the tradition for use in the present? Wouldn't it further be most holy to commemorate our roots in the regular experience of the ritual? Thank You, God, for Your continuous and gracious involvement in our human history. Otherwise, the swinging of the pendulum would seem purposeless. But do we actually need to make the liturgy the same everywhere by rules and regulations? The priesthood of Aaron and/or the priesthood of Melchizedek, isn't this the question underneath?

I further fantasize about hearing the *berakah*, the prayer at the minor elevation, which is the culmination of the Offertory, said in Hebrew by the priest. This is evidently a retained prayer of the earliest Jewish Christians from the synagogue or household *seder* worship service. It was, however, very soon put into languages other than Hebrew in the early Church. Jews still say this prayer, now using almost the same words in Hebrew that we use in the various vernacular voices. As more and more gentile liturgies developed in the Church, which was growing throughout the Empire, this prayer from our earliest birthright remained, but in non-Hebrew voice. Wouldn't it be wonderful and wise to have some memory of our Jewish roots in Jesus' own beloved Temple culture in regular ritual use at our Eucharistic liturgies? There would be a significance in the present world, moral as well as political, as we acknowledge our connection to the People of Israel, the Chosen People. Our own gratitude for our origins would be continuously expressed. So, without saying, "Thank you, God, for sending Jesus to the Chosen People from whom we come," we would be saying exactly that. We could also collaterally do some small recompense for the historic anti-Semitism of our Church in some moments of her liturgical history.

Remembering further that the very word Eucharist means "thank you," we could also thank God for these historical periods in our Tradition. I should like to see, for example, the Lamb of God, the *Agnus Dei* , sung or said in Latin, for much the same reason as I would like to see the *Kyrie* in Greek, or the *Sanctus* in Hebrew; this would viscerally recognize significant parts of our history in the universal Church. There is as great a musical history for these prayers in Latin as there is for the *Kyrie* in Greek. The mind of the Faithful had been capable of understanding the meaning behind the foreign words for centuries; it should have no trouble returning to these reverent references to our history.

I believe that this reclamation of our mysterious tradition would be not only an homage to our past but a reminder of the *Mysterium* which we celebrate. God's ways are not our ways.

18

Saying Mass?

During my years in theological training in the 'seventies there was much emphasis on the necessity of "coming across" during the liturgy. We were taught that it would be very good to silently read the prayers printed in the sacramentary and then to pray aloud, **in our own words**, the prayer of the Church. This is becoming rather old fashioned as more and more the whole Roman Church is moving toward a more regular and less surprising sense of liturgy. A consideration of a thirty-five-year experience in the liturgy as taught in seminaries after Vatican II is a valuable exercise at this point. The validity of the experience does not mean it is normative, but, unforgettably, it did happen with the full support of the universal Roman Catholic Church all over the world for the last half century. Its fruits should be accessible and worth paying attention to as lessons from experience to inform future experience. The lesson of history—those who do not know history are bound to repeat it.

On the days when I have to prepare a homily, there would be a theme—it comes from prayerful consideration of the readings. I found I was discovering the mind of the Church in prayer, reflection, and study for any particular liturgy. It became my practice to prepare four or five hours for a Mass, using the Greek text of the New Testament readings often, especially for exegesis of the gospel. I found that meditating on any foreign language text of scripture brought a lot more food for thought, but in the language in which it was written there is such a connection, again, with the roots of the traditions in Sacred Scripture. I also found that reading a large biblical commentary, like the *Jerome Biblical Commentary,* gave me a lot to think about. Especially helpful to me would be historical considerations. I was profoundly influenced in all this by professors at Weston Jesuit School of Theology, George MacRae, SJ, Stanley Marro, SJ, and Richard Clifford, SJ; the depth of their scholarship was both a challenge and tremendous draw——to know more for the People of God. This becomes a sacred trust.

It was exciting to me; it still is, extremely. It still takes me a few hours to prepare for presiding. (Obviously, in the midst of a large local Jesuit Community, I don't do this daily.) I try to relax into presiding because it is part of the job, to be comfortable at being God's representative. Whereas I used to worry about cramming the preparation into a very busy schedule, I have learned to trust that God will use my efforts and touch whom He will. As I get older, people are more receptive to "words of wisdom" from me. I know that those words, spoken in their hearts by the Spirit Herself, might find congruence with what I might say, but they are heard in the heart through grace. I have no claim on that, exactly, but I do trust it. I find myself growing less self-conscious. It used to be that I felt so deeply the message, both so simple and straightforward, that one need only focus (and not talk), so preaching itself was a chore. I have since come to realize that the job of preaching must include a certain amount of teaching, a certain amount of entertaining, and a certain amount of self-revelation. Those three, in small doses, making four, or at most five, points, seems to be the best bet for me——to make homilies that don't drive the congregation mad. I also find that writing out a sermon doesn't work for me at all, because I get caught up in reading the presentation, losing that vital connection. My Mom wisely told me on the phone, when I called to say that I'd been accepted for ordination to the diaconate, that I should never preach over three minutes. I used to do just that; I am trying to get back to it.

Communication is the life's blood of academics, and so I rely on that learned ability. I preach with a couple of points to keep me on track and try to pay attention to whether or not the congregation is "with me." Sometimes, of course, it is impossible to tell. Then I pray for wisdom, ask that the Holy Spirit will take whatever I do and transform it so that the congregation will hear whatever it is She would have them hear. This is dependence on the promises of Pentecost. It does work. Preaching still takes a lot out of me but it is not so much a fearsome chore anymore.

At any rate, the approach to on-the-spot praying, coupled with keeping a sense of immediacy in preaching, led me to accept the things that were being taught in priestly formation at my time in seminary. Be attentive to both God and the People of God. Be the go-between, the *pontifex*, the bridge-builder. When it came to praying the Preface and Eucharistic Prayer, I found it necessary to come up with something that I could comfortably pray rather than read. I like the Second Eucharistic Prayer and used it as the basis for an "extended canon." This would allow for paying attention to the words as I said them, while paying attention to the breathing of the Holy Spirit in the needs of the community. It's memorized but fluid, the second canon prayed with an open heart.

The Preface is traditionally addressed to God the Father, paying attention to His activity in constant creation, thanking Him for His loving care. The *Epiclesis* and the institution narrative constitute the second part of the Canon; in it we address the Father, reminding Him, and ourselves, of the great gift of Jesus, His Son, by the action of the Holy Spirit. This second part is a continuation of the consideration of God's constant creation through the Son. The third part is about *anamnesis* and the work of the Holy Spirit in the world, especially in the Church. Again, the prayer is addressed to the Father, asking Him to continue His constant care through the Spirit, which Jesus left for us when He said, "Peace, I give you... Receive the Holy Spirit; go and baptize the whole world in the name of the Father and of the Son and of the Holy Spirit."

Following is a transcript of the Canon that I have prayed. It is quite similar to Eucharistic Prayer II, but a little longer. It starts with an expanded Preface, moves through the *epiclesis* (calling down the Spirit on the gifts) to the institution narrative (using the words of the Lord fairly strictly from the text because they are universal and sacred in that), through the *anamnesis* (remembering that it is, in, through, and of Christ, that we are the People of God). This third part of the canon includes prayers for the world, the Church, leaders of both, the sick and the dead, and all present at the liturgy. It ends with the Major Elevation and the Great Amen.

The new insistence on uniformity in liturgy and the consequent abhorrence of emotion is a swing of the pendulum. As we become more and more rigid, we seem to return to a Church of the Pharisees. Fearful of offending God by making ritual *faux pas,* we become intent on noticing the ritual imperfections of others. The "gotcha squad," or ritual observation police, are a strange extrapolation of one scourge of our era. The absolute necessity of paying attention to political correctness even in prayer cripples many who are fearful of the repercussions of offending the righteousness spies. This stifling of creativity makes a whitened sepulcher of correct liturgy. Without allowing room for the Spirit, we deny the power of the *epiclesis,* we denigrate that very thing we do when we extend our hands over the sacred species and ask that the Holy Spirit descend onto them. "Let Your Holy Spirit come upon these so that they may become, for us, the Body and the Blood of our Lord Jesus Christ." To consider too stringently that this miracle depends on our scrupulously correct repetition of the words and actions is demeaning to our faith in the reality of just Who it is Who is the High Priest.

19

A New Canon for the Church of the Apocalypse

Blessed are You, Lord God of all Creation, King of the Universe, Prince of Peace, Everlasting Father, Wonder, Counselor. You have given us this bread to offer, fruit of the earth and the work of human hands. It represents our daily needs; let it be our spiritual food.

R Blessed be God, forever.

Blest, too, are You, Lord God of all Consolation, for you have given us this wine to offer. It represents our joy in fellowship; it will become our spiritual drink.

R Blessed be God, forever.

Pray, my brothers and sisters,... and for all the Church.

[Say here the Offertory Prayer.]

The Preface

The Lord is with you.

R   And also with You.

Let us lift up our hearts.

R   We have lifted them up to the Lord.

Let us give thanks to the Lord our God.

R   It is right and just.

Father, it is right for us to be here to praise You and thank You. And so, we do. We bless You, Lord, for all the times and ways that you have blessed us. We thank You for the lights of the sky and the lights on the earth. We thank You for all the blessings that you have showered on us: the clouds, the trees, the fish of the sea, all the creatures of the earth.

We praise You for putting this planet in its course around the sun. We bless you for separating the sea and the land and for putting Your hand in the water and making life on this planet. We thank You for all the blessings that You have showered on us. We praise You for separating us into male and female and for planting in us the desire for union, a desire in which is hidden the very mystery of life itself. You have given us power over the preservation of our race and dominion over the planet. We bless You for speaking to men and to women, helping us to know what we are to do with Your gifts.

We thank You for speaking to Mohammed and to the Buddha, and for speaking Your truth to our father, Abraham and to his wife, Sarah, to their children and their children's children, from generation unto generation. We praise You for speaking to all the patriarchs, to Abraham, Isaac, and Jacob, and to the matriarchs, Sarah, Rebecca, Leah, and Rachel. We praise you for speaking to kings and queens like David, Solomon, and Esther. We praise you for speaking to the prophets: Isaiah, Jeremiah, Ezekiel. We bless You for speaking to priests like Aaron and Melchizedek, and to Zechariah, the old priest of Jerusalem and to his wife,

Elizabeth, and to their son, John, the last prophet of the old covenant, who saw so clearly how small are we and how great You are. He preached a baptism of sin and repentance. We praise You, too, because in the fullness of time, You spoke Your Word, through the angel Gabriel, to the young woman betrothed to the carpenter, Joseph. We praise You because You waited for her to respond to You before You sent Him into the World, the Word who would redeem us.

We praise You for all that He said and did. We praise You for His learning to pray from His mother and learning a trade from His father. We bless You for the gentleness of His voice and the tenderness of His eyes. We praise You for the way He touched people, healing them out of time and space. We praise You for His new Baptism in the Holy Spirit. We praise You for all Your gifts; first, last, and always, we praise You for this Jesus. We praise You for His birth in a stable, His death on a cross, and for His resurrection from the tomb. We praise You as men and women have praised You for centuries as we say:

Ka-dosh, ka-dosh, ka-dosh A-do-nai Tz'va-ot, M'lochal Ha-a-retz K'vo-do

Holy, holy, holy, Lord, God of hosts. Heaven and earth are full of Your glory. Hosannah in the highest. Blessed is He who comes in the name of the Lord. Hosannah in the highest.

[Here are said the words and done the action of the Epiclesis.]

Father, You are holy. All creation gives You praise. We, Your people, wish to be holy, and so we ask You to send Your Holy Spirit upon these gifts to make them holy, so that they may become for us the Body and Blood of Your Son, our Lord and Brother, Jesus Christ.

[The Institution Narrative.]

When He was at table with His friends, He took bread. He blessed it, broke it, and gave it to His disciples saying:

Take, eat, this is my Body which is given up for you.

He took the cup, blessed it, lifted up His eyes and said: Take this cup of My Blood, the new and eternal covenant. It will be shed for you and for many for the forgiveness of sins.

Do this as a remembrance of Me.

Let's proclaim the mystery of our Faith:

R   Christ has died, Christ has risen, Christ will come again.

And so, Father, we remind You of all that He said and did. We remind You as if You needed reminding. Out of time and space He did miracles because people asked Him. He made the blind see, the deaf hear, the mute speak. He even raised the dead. We remind You of how much He loved those who were His own in the world. We remind You, as if You needed reminding, that it was in His love and understanding that Jesus sent the Holy Spirit. We remind You that we still need the Holy Spirit and we dare to ask You, in Jesus' name: give us Your Holy Spirit. Fill the air we breathe with the Breath of God; let us feel the Wings of Wisdom. Put Your fire, wind, and water into our very souls.

[The anamnesis words and action.]

In memory of His death and resurrection, Father, we offer You this life-giving Bread, this saving Cup. We thank You for counting us worthy to gather around this altar and to praise You. May all of us who are gathered in this one Body and Blood be brought together in unity by the Holy Spirit.

Father, look with favor on our troubled world. Help our leaders to make and keep the peace. Help us all to reverence Your gifts, different races, different species.

Father, bless our Church. Make her a leaven of Your justice and Your mercy, Your kingdom on the earth. Bless the leaders: ... our pope, ... our bishop, and all the leaders of this holy Church, with the entire people Your Son has gained for you.

Bless our loved ones who are not here...; give them Faith, Hope, and Charity. Bless our sick ...; give them health of mind, body, and spirit. Bless our enemies with Your holy Wisdom. Bless our beloved dead ....; bring them and all the faithful departed into the light of Your presence. Bless each of us here with the gifts of the Holy Spirit that we need so that we might freely be ourselves, that we might love one another, that we might seek You all our days. Call us all home one day that we might praise You forever, together with Mary the Virgin Mother of God, with Joseph, the apostles and martyrs, and all those holy men and women who have done Your will throughout the ages. May we praise You in union with them and give You glory through Your Son, Jesus the Christ. It is through Him and with Him and in Him all glory and honor are Yours, almighty Father, for ever and ever.

R Amen.

This Canon is not significantly different from the many Eucharistic Prayers in the Sacramentary. It is essentially, as stated above, the Second Eucharistic Prayer. But it has the advantage for me of being owned enough that I can pray it, getting in all the necessary parts, without reading them. Using almost the same words every time but not being so scrupulous as to lose the congregation. In another period, I realize, I might easily have been one of those scrupulous priests who kept repeating the words of consecration, trying to be sure to *mean* them. This insight into the *drama* of the Eucharistic Prayer is a discovery of a lifetime for me. Scrupulosity about exactly correct wording is a diabolical distraction. We must trust God. People tell me that I help them to pray the prayer. I beg the Lord to help me not to lead the people astray, not to get in His way. I am humbled by praying this prayer for the people, for God's Church, addressing God intimately.

Because the prayer's progress is in my mind, I can pray with eyes closed. This is a great advantage for connecting with God. People say that it seems like I mean what I say, rather than reading what I am told. My brother once told me that he appreciated the way I spoke to God, concentrating on God, and, on the other hand, spoke to him (and the rest of the congregation), concentrating on him (them). The first comment has a certain naïve quality, which makes me think that they are, perhaps, telling a profound truth. The second really humbles me. It threatens some others. May God, in His goodness, protect the Church from the personal pitfalls of her priests, like me! But may He help us to know what risks to take.

There is a danger in doing liturgy in this way

The fact is that doing what one finds in prayer as the way the Lord would have him preside will win him some animosity. There is a fundamental problem with anyone standing out in his functioning as a priest. There is the fact that someone might not understand exactly where the priest is coming from and, rather than ask, might react. This is an understandable human response. After all, Catholics often feel that they have no say in the way the Church functions in their lives; it is a residue, perhaps, of years of living under the ideological control of the priesthood of Aaron. Most of us have had an experience or two of feeling that we don't like what is going on in the parish or the school but we have no way of doing anything about it. So, when someone doesn't like what the priest is doing at Mass, s/he might respond heavy-handedly. What do I do in that situation? I try to take the criticism seriously, to see whence it comes and ask myself, as honestly as I can: "Is this criticism a correct one? Is there something that I have overlooked or misconstrued? Is this person's criticism normative for this congregation?" Then, one way or the other I pray about what my response should be, trying to be true to my understanding of what God is asking of me as both cult priest of Aaron and as His priest of Melchizedek.

Discernment of spirits can be done with the help of a spiritual companion or director. Finding out whether God wants us to do more in serving His people is necessary for anyone who would feel called to do so. The Church is duty-bound to protect herself from heresy. So anyone who does anything outside the norm will be questioned. Doing anything outside the norm requires courage. But courage is not enough. Having some certitude that God is with us in living or practicing outside the norm, being "counter-cultural" in other words, is needed, if one would authentically allow difference in himself to show itself in service. We need some assurance that it is asked by God and not merely human folly.

The Canon which I use really takes little risk. But it does take into account some of the needs of the people for the priest to really *seem* to be connected both to them and to God. In *Acts* 11 we learn of Peter's conflict with Paul over the inclusion of the uncircumcised, the non-Jews, into the Church. Paul outlines his argument often, as in *Philippians* 3. Peter's inspiration comes in a dream of non-Kosher foods being offered by angels. He understands. God has made us all for Himself. So, acknowledging that God has spoken, as the author of the *Letter to the Hebrews* says, in many ways in times past but has now brought salvation in the best Word God should ever speak, His Son, Jesus, salvation for us all, we must all trust something inside, which tells us to take care of God's people. Sometimes we must preach without words, sometimes with. The Eucharistic Prayer must be in words and they should be the right words, but they should also be from the heart. We have to do something to make it so.

So the point becomes: Do your best, priest of God, to be both true to the demands of God in the exercise of your duties as a son of Aaron, and kind in the service of God's people in that same exercise as a priest according to the order of Melchizedek. Do not give up your gifts because they bother somebody who deems himself righteous or because you are expected to conform—unless God asks that of you—because grace builds on nature, God's grace on our nature!

20

Penance

Now about Penance, this is a difficult thing, because the tradition is so very strong and the need so very constant. We know that the *Mexica*, or Aztecs, had a tradition of confession once in one's life. It was practiced long before the arrival of anyone from the Court of Carlos Quinto (Charles V, Holy Roman Emperor, Charles I, King of Spain, grandson of Ferdinand and Isabella) arrived in Tenochtitlan. So the tradition, more universal than Judaeo-Christian, acknowledges the human need to share guilt or shame with another human being. The need has led in our own day to the fields of Counseling, Psychology, and Psychiatry as well as many pseudo-fields of sixth-sense intuitive intellection. The need to unburden is surely well-established.

A significant problem for Catholic priests today rests in this, that the move from absolute secrecy, afforded the penitent *incognito* in the old confessional boxes, has been given up for a more interpersonal face to face encounter. The priest now has a sense that he is not supposed to dispense the Church's grace with anonymous abandon. He is supposed to engage those who choose to sit and face him. The problem is that this has become a "counseling session," which demands more of a priest than his training may have prepared him for.

The Sacrament of Penance must have to do more with the penitent's desire to face the Lord squarely and admit his/her faults and sinful tendencies. This is healthier than keeping our faults from ourselves. Admission before God is tantamount to honesty with self and dependence on God's grace. This is a ministerial objective of the confessional encounter, to encourage the encounter, or re-encounter, with God. By the ministry of the Church the priest helps the penitent to admit, to confess, to ask forgiveness, and, ultimately, to realize that God's forgiveness is much more powerful than anything any other human being can offer. The words, the blessing, the hug—not only is it the Father who has forgiven when asked, but the Holy Spirit hovering, whispering, hugging, giving the Church the wings of human contact through me to the penitent. An angelic presence makes all things new for her/him in Jesus' name and in view of Jesus' sacrifice. But the ritual is the ministry of the Church, not the personal healing ministry of the priest, and so there is need for less confusion about just what are the sacrament's boundaries.

Divine forgiveness might not wipe out the consequences of our actions but it can, and we believe it does, wipe out our eternal guilt. The sense of being unforgivable is the unbearable burden that the priest is supposed to help lift. Thus, a mystery of God's love is held up as a holy ministry, an inviolable trust, even before its development by the Ionian monks into a rather introspective public human endeavor to admit responsibility for wrongdoing or hurtful tendencies. (Some would say it became, for too long a while, overly public and punitive.) God's grace through the ministry of the Church is here dependent on the attitude of the penitent, but the channel remains the ministry of the Church through the action of the Church's minister. This sounds Melchizedekian enough.

Here, however, appear the horns of a dilemma. Some would think that the priest, according to the admonition of the evangelical accounts, is supposed to decide guilt and render judgment, in God's name, about whether or not the penitent can be forgiven. The texts most often used to support this role of the priest are from *John* and

Matthew: "whose sins you forgive, they are forgiven them; whose sins you retain, they are retained." (*John* 20: 23) and "If you bind them on earth, they will be bound in heaven. If you loose them on earth they will be loosed in heaven." (*Matthew* 18:18,19)

This has always bothered me, the idea that some should be judged "unforgivable." So, using the tools I learned in biblical exegesis in the school of Theology, I went to the Greek original to pray over it and to discern what it could mean. To "retain" someone's sins seemed beyond the ken of the English vernacular in which I have learned most of what I know of Church History, Canon Law, Biblical Criticism, Psychology, and Sacramental Theology. There is only the vague image of keeping, "retaining," one's sins as in a kind of prison.

Behold, however, the treasure of studying the original text! In the Matthean story it says: What you bind (*desete*) on the earth will be bound in heaven (*dedemena*) and what you loose (*lusete*) on the earth will be loosed in heaven (*lelumena*). Both of these images suggest a positive result of confession. If a person is bound up by his/her sin, the apostles can loosen the bonds. And, if, on the other hand, a person is falling to pieces as a result of her/sin sin, the apostles can hold them together. The Johannine image says: If you pardon (*aphete*) someone's sins they are pardoned (*apheontai*). If you check or overcome (*kratete*) someone's sins they are checked or overcome (*kekratentai*). If you take off someone's burden, it is taken off; if you empower someone, he/she is empowered.

So, both narratives, which **establish** the precedents for the sacrament of penance suggest two ways in which the Church might relieve the penitent of the burden of his/her sins. There is no suggestion in the Greek, whereas there is in the Latin (*retinere*), that the Church might decide to not forgive, to not unburden, to not loosen, to not bind up, to not support the penitent. The temptation to hold the guilty at arm's length and lord it over them, as it were, is more consonant with a sacerdotal power directly related to a kind of im-

perial or papal authority structure. This sounds quite Aaronic—the
rules are paramount! Adherence is required; resistance is futile. That
tradition seems to have arisen late in the history of the Western
Church, the Latin Church of Rome, with the influence of those austere Irish monks from Iona. Consider this: any island off that coast
of Ireland would naturally engender austerity in response to both
God and nature! They were great preservers of so much of classical
culture, and they were proponents of individual confession—both
great achievements. It fits into a medieval mindset wherein the
Church is the protector of the widow and the orphan against the
power of the nobility.

But guilt has a way of becoming a painful tool when remorse is
demanded but not rewarded. In public and private venues, guilt, as
the key to acceptance in society, becomes a way to separate ourselves into *quasi-castes;* but when guilt cannot be assuaged, the penitent is forever held less than human in his/her own eyes. Remorse
or sorrow for making separations from God is what penance demands. If someone realizes remorse for having hurt God or any
other, it is a great grace, not to be denied. Although the grace might
not remove the consequences of his or her past actions in a person's
life, the removal of guilt can allow a reconnection with the all-for-
giving God .

The recommendation of the Master is to be kind. The encyclical of Pope Benedict on Love recommends a deep commitment to
emulating this divine trait. The most recent Code of Canon Law
seems to have reinforced this interpretation when it reduced the
number of impediments to forgiveness. The experience of history,
furthermore, recommends holding a heavy threat over the wayward
faithful; it may just be a thing of history, to show us how good ideas
can become bad practices. Perhaps the priest of today must pray a
good deal about how he is best exercising his role in the confessional.

The Aaronic tradition might suggest a more levitical approach,
to be like a Sadducee or a Pharisee when reminding the faithful that

they are far from deserving God's mercy and love. The Melchizedekian tradition might otherwise suggest letting history take care of itself, you be perfect like the heavenly Father is perfect—spend everything for the beloved, forgive, and pray a lot.

A caveat

There has occurred in recent years a terrible reason for collective guilt in the Roman Church in North America, as well as in many other places. Both the scandal of clerical sexual abuse of minors and the self-protective response of some of the hierarchy has led to a reinforcement of the self-crippling feeling of being less than human if one is a cleric. The attitude is, of course, reinforced by the reaction of the American hierarchy, which insists that all priests attend meetings and sign papers which say in effect, "I understand and agree that touching anyone, or any interaction between myself and any potentially suspicious directee, penitent, counselee, or child, behind closed doors, is tantamount to an accusable offense and, therefore, I will never be alone or be intimate with any clerical client. Nor will I allow a child to think or feel inappropriate things about me." This arrangement leads to a sense of indefensible sinfulness on the part of the priests, so much so that the institutional Church finds counsel to guard itself against the possible improprieties of its priests. The guilt is compounded. The priest feels as though he might inadvertently do something kind in response to a wounded penitent, patient, student, or client, which might cause the Church to be sued. Moreover, in order to protect the faithful from such inadvertent "sloppiness," the dioceses, with the help of the Virtus and Praesidium programs and relying on the documents provided by Virtus and Praesidium, have asked the priest (and all other employees of the Church's ministries) to regard touch and intimacy as questionable techniques in the exercise of ministry. This especially redounds to the exercise of compassion in the confessional. Face to face, and yet, now no longer empowered to exercise human tenderness, the priest is asked simply to dispense grace—somehow unearthly, somewhat inhuman, effective without being affective. While face to face, yet not trained to be a counselor, we are without the normal human tools of kindness, which the Master used so often in a counter-cultural way. He had converse and even tactile intercourse with prostitutes and tax collectors.

I think, perhaps, this double-edged sword needs to be reexamined. In the meantime, perhaps, we can rely on the Beatitudes, which have the Master say, "Blessed are those who mourn ... the merciful ... those who seek justice.....and blessed are you, when people utter every kind of slander against you because of what you do in My name, yours is the kingdom of heaven." In the meantime, perhaps, a will to imitate the counter-cultural Christ, will mean taking risks, being tender, even though some might claim that we consort with sinners.

21

Recessional

The differences between the priesthood according to the order of Aaron, the priesthood according to the order of Levi, and the priesthood according to the order of Melchizedek, become quite clear when we look in the Book for rules. The Old Testament is full of rules and regulations for the priests, sons of Aaron and the sons of Levi. There is very little mention of Melchizedek in either the Old or New Testaments.

It becomes rather evident, then, that the cultic priesthood of the hereditary office holders, Aaron's sons, is mostly about attendance at the Presence focused in the Ark of the Covenant; that of the sons of Levi has to do with attention to the details of worship in the outer courts, the cleansing of utensils, oblations, etc.

The role of Aaron's sons seems to correlate with what has come into our era as the priest who attends to the rites closest to the Holy of Holies, which is the Presence. The Presence cannot be held down by our rites, but we attend to the Trinity in different ways, more to the Christ in the Eucharist and in the tabernacle, more to the Holy Spirit in sacraments of Baptism, Confirmation, Marriage, Ordination, Anointing, and more to the Father in Penance. Even though virtually all of the prayers in all the rites are addressed to the Father, about the work or history of the other Two, there is a sense of co-operation with one or other of the Trinity in the different rites of the Church. We see how They operate, or with what works of the Church we are to cooperate better, because we have these seven sacraments.

The diaconal role, the service role, of the Levitical priesthood has been transformed in our era into attending to more practical needs, preaching, visiting the sick, taking care of the material needs of the sacraments. By need, the role of the deacon has developed even to presiding at the Mass of the Pre-sanctified, as it is called in Eastern Churches; the term means Eucharist, without the Eucharistic Prayer (and consecration)—or "Mass" presided over by an ordained priest — from which the faithful are sent (*missi* or *missae*) fortified by communion even without that consecrating prayer of a priest. The deacons also preside at Baptism, Benediciton, and Wake services and the prayers at the graveside. So the diaconate greatly resembles the priesthood of the Tribe of Levi in our present era, as well sometimes as that of the priests of Aaron. So what we have been speaking of as two priesthoods appears to have a triple biblical history in Melchizedek, Aaron, and Levi, although there is a conflation in the diaconate, at times, of the traditions of Aaron and Levi.

The modern equivalents of priesthood have roots in the words and works of Jesus. He did choose the seventy-two others according to one evangelist (*Luke* 10) to aid the apostles in a practical carrying of the burden. Some think of these as *proto deacons*. But the Master gave us the most important gloss on the history of the Hebraic priesthoods and their transmogrification into the Christian era, when in *John*, He washed the feet of the disciples, telling them that their role, like His, will be to serve! According to the Epistle to the Hebrews, we are, all of us, called to participate in Jesus' High Priesthood "according to the Order of Melchizedek."

"I want mercy not sacrifice."

"Do you love Me? Feed my Lambs." This Johannine (*John* 21) passage that always seems, in the vernacular, to be very strong because of its repetitions, becomes much stronger in the Greek because of the differences within those repetitions. Not only is this a triple Hebraic emphasis, but a complicated and linguistically beautiful story told in poetic ironies. Jesus asks Peter about his affection for Him, and with the positive answer He tells Peter to feed His lambs.

This image, even for us, so removed from rural sheep herding, is a very tender one. The cute white or black lamb, fuzzy with pink parts, held in the arms like a baby, being fed by a bottle. Very nice! But the Master changes the terms when He asks again. Peter's shocked second response is greeted by "tend My sheep." This image is also accessible to us, a shepherd on a hill or in a corral with his baaaa-ing sheep, bigger, seeming somewhat less intelligent, less clean, less little, less cute. But we get the point. The third time Jesus changes the verb from affection to love. Peter doesn't quite get it. He seems annoyed this time, when he says, "You *know* that I love you." John has Jesus adroitly change the meaning by mixing the nouns and verbs, putting the more caring verb (feed) together with the uglier noun (sheep). Now the image is of tenderly bottle-feeding the sheep who are more unruly, less cuddly. The point is rabbinically absolute. The role of the leader is to serve absolutely, loving the unrewarding recipient as one would the adorable.

Now, when we pray about our ordination, there are many images, numbingly humbling images. We are to take the place of Christ, we are to represent the historical apostolic institution, we are to shepherd the flock. These are replete with pride-filled memories of how the priests of old led Christendom to its splendid place in western history. But it is very good to consider this test of our understanding. Recall that day of the imposition of hands. What did we hear? You are a priest forever, according to the order of (1) Aaron, (2) Levi, or (3) Melchizedek. (Choose one.)

Further, when we were ordained deacon. Remember? "Receive the book of the Gospels. Believe what you read. Preach what you believe. Practice what you preach" (or something quite like that). There is room for believing that we are the modern-day equivalents of the sons of Aaron and Levi, because history/Tradition has given this to us. There is, however, also a moral requirement that we assume the role of the priest/king Melchizedek.

Deep inside ourselves we must also remember the Matthean proscription: Call no one Teacher except the Messiah, no one Father except the Father who is in heaven. Our desire to take a place of honor is a natural one—but one to be put in proper perspective against the backdrop of Christ's ordination into the Order of Melchizedek (in the seventh chapter of Hebrews) at His spilling of His blood. We must make no mistake about this. We have chosen the Lord. We are not promised an easy or a respectable life! We are promised pie in the sky when we die. We must, of all people, keep our eye on the prize, fight the good fight. Be kind, be love, be Christ to all and sundry.

Two standards

Consider the differences between the *Book of Leviticus* and the *Epistle to the Romans* or contrast *Deuteronomy* and *Thessalonians*. There really does seem to be some conflict, two polarities, in thinking about how the priests are to lead the people of God. I guess this is an eternal as well as an internal conflict. St. Ignatius of Loyola contrasted "Two earthly leaders" and their "Two Standards" in the middle of the *Spiritual Exercises*. In the introduction to these meditations, he says that the leaders are both beautiful, very attractive, but calling their "troops" to different ends. The "two standards" refer to the banners carried in medieval conflicts as the battle flags, the call to arms. On them the goals of the princes are symbolized. Satan as the one leader has a banner which advertises plenty, power, and prestige—the promises he makes to his followers. Christ's standard offers the opposing values, poverty, powerlessness, and humiliation. The meditations place in extreme focus just what are the deepest desires of our hearts. Now, I do not mean to contrast the Aaronic and Melchizedekian constructs as one being diabolical and one angelic, nor even that that they are contradictory approaches. I mean, rather, to suggest again that there is a conflict within each of us between the desire to do good in God's name to and for individuals in exercising tenderness, and to and for the people more generally in giving direction. There is an opening in both motives for the priest to lose his way, to try to overpower, to fix by controlling, rather than to serve in a humble way. The important thing for the individual priest is to keep his heart pure as best he can, to make his mind follow the directives of a heart united with God, to risk humiliation in order to follow the High Priest's example. Whether acting as a cultic presider or as a personal director, since the two roles collide when we officiate at sacramental rituals, we must be first the representative of the Christ and second the representative of the Church. I know this will bother some, because it should be that the two are ineluctably intertwined. True enough, but the person who is the priest is human enough to divide them and sometimes to divide them completely—to the detriment of his fulfilling his high office.

It is interesting to note that the term "bishop," which comes from the Greek *episcopos,* means "over-seer" or "over-looker," but the role is said to come from that of the *apostoloi,* the apostles. The meaning, "sent ones," is quite close to one of the traditional meanings of the Mass, a term which comes, at least in part, from the admonition at the end of the Tridentine Liturgy: *Ite, missa est,* which can be seen to mean, "Go, you are sent (as apostles) into the world." [To be sure, it can also be translated somewhat eisegetically, "Go, in peace, the Mass is ended."]

A couple of modern writers of note have contrasted the two motives within the media-saturated activities of the Vatican. Herbert Haag in *Upstairs, Downstairs: Did Jesus Want a Two-Class Church?* (Crossroads, 1998) says that there has arisen a two-class society within the

Church, the ordained and the laity. He got into quite a bit of trouble with the watchdogs of heresy because of some of his conclusions, but the basic premise is pellucidly clear. I believe that the contrast in the roles of the two traditional biblical orders of priesthood is at the root of the perception.

Garry Wills in his *Papal Sin: Structures of Deceit* (Doubleday, 2000) posits a real threat to the holiness of the whole Church in the need to protect the papacy as a world power running on wealth, politics, and pride. He does, however, accept the historical reality as one within which God's Church is still developing. It is the context within which we still operate.

Hans Kung in his *The Catholic Church: A Short History* (Modern Library Chronicles, 2001) reduces the difficulty to polar opposites within the structures of the Vatican. He suggests that there is a camp which protects the Curia with all the ammunition, keeping a hold on the wealth, power, and prestige for the structures of Vatican politics. He contrasts this with the loving leadership of some Bishops of Rome as they have developed their place over time and within history through the art of compromise. Making do with what was possible in the context of their times, some popes built a solid power block for moral leadership within their worlds. He, too, is unopposed, apparently, to the idea of an historically developed papacy which has the assurance of loving involvement from the Holy Spirit.

It appears that not only is there a contrast between clergy and laity, but also a contrast between those who *protect* the central leadership from those who would dialog with it and those who see God's action in the world as more diversified. These latter see the Priesthood of Christ, the priesthood of the order of Melchizedek, as *shared* by the will and power, the working of the Holy Spirit, with the whole People of God, grace on nature, some clergy, some laity, gifted, and to be treasured for the revelation shared by God through them.

"Whitened sepulchers" (*Matthew* 23:26) is a traditional and poetically profound translation in Jesus' denunciation of the pharisaical who would keep rules to the detriment of their souls. The image of pretty white tombs full of rotting flesh and bones is harsh, but, like so many rabbinical images, clear and recognizable, strong, undeniable, and quite cutting to the heart of the matter. It is ironic that so much of the fabric of the interior of St. Peter's Basilica is covered with white marble tombs of dead popes. Many of the papal tombs, by their own recommendations, however, have images suggesting that the dead pope was a great man in the eyes of the world while he lived, but now he lies here rotting under the beauty. A great and holy pope could see that all life ends and that one's life should have been lived well because, in the end, we are all dead. The implication: we all face the Lord and must answer for our choices. I believe the deepest desire of the greatest holders of the papacy is for all of the Christian world to be populated with men and women who love God with everything in them, and their neighbor as themselves—to the best of their ability. This must include us priests, I should think.

Conclusion

So it seems we are trying to say very few things. One: the concern that the ordained have for the buildings and structures of religion are part of the cultural job of the priest. It grew as the result of a relationship of the cultic priest to the people and the ecclesial structure, which developed within the history of the People of God. Thus, the desire to be right, to have good order, to see things done according to rules, each of these is part of the priesthood of Aaron, and can be found in the diaconal traditions of the priests of Levi. The concerns of the earth, the Church in space and time, people seeming righteous within the community, these concerns belong to that part of our priesthood which comes from history and people. The privilege of entering the Holy of Holies, of serving inside the sanctuary, is full of honor and dignity. That all comes from the happenstance of history, a *result* of the role that priests play between the people and their God; it is our heritage.

However, the more important part of the call is that which would concern us with carrying out the great work of the Priesthood of Melchizedek. This is the priesthood in which Jesus is the High Priest, according to the *Letter to the Hebrews*. He does what Melchizedek did; He feeds us bread and wine, nourishing us with His body and quenching our thirst with His blood. To give of ourselves in service is the noblest call of the Church, a clarion call through the ministry of the Church, from the mouth of God.

It is of utmost importance that the ordained priests see with absolute clarity the differences between these roles. We need to withstand the tempestuous voices, both within and without, which would have us lord it over anyone. We must serve as a slave; we must pour ourselves out. The example is clearer for us than for any other role in the Church. The cross is our badge of membership in the priesthood of Christ. That is the one that counts, the priesthood of Christ.

I would offer a couple of *vade mecum*'s, as kôans almost, for the ordained:

> ▶ There is *no priest but Jesus*. (We participate in *His* priesthood, according to *Hebrews*. We are not to call one another Father or Teacher, according to *Matthew*.)

> ▶ I am called to serve according to both the orders of Aaron and Melchizedek as a result of my involvement in the *service of God's People in history*.

> ▶ *Nothing matters* more than how I love His people individually and communally, **except** how I love God. In the final reckoning *this counts*.

> ▶ The way I preside and live my life should come from both the head and the heart in union with God. *In my very self I must find the harmony of both orders* in order to better serve God and neighbor.

There are many rules that have arisen over centuries. There is Canon Law. There are the rules of the consecrated, vowed religious. There are diocesan norms. There is a lot to consider for the priest so he can look in the mirror and say I am doing the best I can. But the inner freedom to be one with God through the ministry of the Church is paramount for all Christians, the priest included. The inner freedom should help him to be more like Jesus. His willingness to ask for Wisdom, that inner freedom, bolstered by the prayers of the Church, should lead him to greater inner freedom, peace, and kindness, which will allow him to recognize the face of Jesus when he passes through the veil of time and space himself, when his own particular encounter with the Second Coming puts him beyond the trials of trying to be another Christ, when Jesus, the One Christ, finally says, "Come into the place prepared for you before time began." The priest will recognize the face of Jesus because of the kindness he shall have shown the other Christs who will have asked his help all during his priestly life, more than for the order he will have imposed on nature.

A global corollary

Conservative clerical movements thrive throughout the inter-religious community. Ayatollahs, rabbis, archpriests, televangelists, curialists in Rome or Canterbury, and lay advocates of religious righteousness demand conformity to the whims of the various high commands. Threats and full-scale excommunications against any who don't agree with certain decrees dangerously threaten the liberating worship of God. A consequent loss of reverence for the freedoms pointed out by St. Paul in *Romans* and his other epistles is growing cancerous; with increasing venom interior freedom is denigrated as deconstructive of church, mosque, synagogue, and temple. An era of angry righteousness was deplored by God in *Ezekiel* 34. God said how fed-up He was with the shepherds because they take care of themselves and their prerogatives first. Something like it seems to happen repeatedly, but the present righteous moment is

particularly painful. The reign of an anti-Christ is the repressive dec-
laration of clerical overlord after clerical overlord, resulting in vast
hatreds and exclusive repressive sects in every sector, seeking freedom from pain by punishing those who see things differently. This is
a disaster, crying to heaven for another prophet to show us the way.

22

Postlude

Recently I was present for the ordination ceremonies for the local provinces of the Society of Jesus in New York, at Fordham University, the very chapel in which I was ordained thirty-two years before, almost to the day. There were a few tears shed by many. My own included memories of those in my own pantheon of departed, beloved family members who were present on that day. So much loss in one's lifetime! It can change the backdrop for everything, even Faith.

There were so many things that were so similar to my own ordination day and some significant changes. We were twelve then, this group was only four, but they seemed to be very fine and already tested young men. They come later in life than we had; these were mostly accomplished professional men when they began the journey to this altar as Jesuits a decade or so earlier. They're a good bit older and, please God, they are wiser, at least than I was. The most recent attention to the chapel's infrastructure made the building more substantial in its appearance; the floor had no wooden temporariness, the pews didn't wobble, the altar, pulpit, and presidential seat seemed like they were more permanent. But the music was more sophisticated, too, the choir sounding much more professional, the melodies so much more mature than those of the earlier vernacular liturgical music. Remember, so many things that were so much less beautiful than the Gregorian Revival of the post World War II era or, indeed of the Lutheran or Anglican traditions, which we Romans were reluctant to borrow in those isolationist days! But there seems to be a growth in the Church, even based in the still virulent antagonisms in the American Church between the self-identified conservative and liberal combatants, the dialogue has come to some peaceful and beautiful compromises. I think this indicates the cooperative and actual graces of the Holy Spirit Who blows where She will. Creative Church members seem to be focusing on praising God in beauty rather than on self-aggrandizing agonies over what must never be done again, namely anything which does not comfort me and my allies! Remember Pope Paul's famous apology to the artists when he made reference to the demands that he and his predecessors had made on artists, that they make art and music which reminded them of the days of their youth in the not so effervescent Church of the early twentieth-century liturgical revivals. He'd apologized for having imposed "as it were, a cloak of lead."

There were other differences. The priesthood of Aaron seemed so to be stressed, mentioned a number of times throughout the Liturgy. The priesthood of Melchizedek was not mentioned. There was a lot said about the interrelationships between the hierarchical Church and the Society of Jesus. When I was ordained three decades earlier, the instruction included a promise articulated by Terence Cardinal Cooke, the then ordaining prelate; he asked, "Do you promise your Ordinary obedience and respect?" The present ordaining prelate, Cardinal Edward Egan, asked, "Will you respect and obey the diocesan bishop and your duly constituted religious superiors?" This, too, was quite a change.

There were, however, women who read the first two readings, and women who brought up the gifts. There were laymen who read the prayer of the faithful and who also brought up gifts. There were men and women in the choir. So some things were different, some things the same.

The only really significant change was the one which reiterates the claim of Archbishop Rembert Weakland that the *sanctuary* has been renamed the *presbyterium*. The realm of the priestly caste is again gaining a kind of medieval dominance. The relegation of the role of the laity in the liturgy becomes a comfortable *rentrenchment*. The advances in this re-establishment in history of the mysterious service-priesthood of Jesus *as He set it up (?)*, perhaps most eloquently in the Holy Thursday soliloquies of St. John's Gospel, are being subsumed under the need for order in a chaotic world. The Church is involved in a life which becomes history; it is there that we find God. But is Christ not always calling us to solidarity in His self-emptying? The ways in which we risk dealing with the messy consequences of Vatican II are still plaguing us. We still want to give them up in order to be comfortable in the orderliness of compliance with regulations. We must not, because those realizations were in consequence of listening to the Wind, attending to the grace of the Holy Spirit. Her Wisdom should not be denied.

There must be some room for reconsideration of the advances made by Vatican II and its aftermath, even though it might be "proven" that this or that Council Father did not mean to establish a high tolerance for difference and creativity. Further, even though it might be shown that many laity really like the authoritarian presence of curial bureaucrats on the world stage, and even though some hierarchical leaders are appealing men. We must not lose sight of what we so urgently accepted as the direct intervention of the Holy Spirit into the life of the Church, the breathing of the Living God into the lungs of the People of God a new song. We can reject only to our peril the advances brought about by Grace.

The Priesthood of Melchizedek is, after all, the priesthood of Christ made manifest in history in the life of the Church; both before and after the historical reality of Christ Jesus on earth, the Holy

Spirit was the Spirit of Wisdom. This Spirit is the primary presence of God that we claim in all the sacraments except, perhaps, in the Eucharist, although even there we call down the Spirit onto the gifts on the altar in the *epiclesis*. We pray to the Father in all sacraments, but we claim the blessings of the Holy Spirit in Baptism, Confirmation, Orders, Matrimony, Anointing, and Penance. We profess belief in this mysterious and constant Companion, the Advocate, the Paraclete. We dare not relegate Her leading us into self-understanding, afforded by *inspiration,* to a secondary or tertiary spot in our self-understanding as the followers of Christ the High Priest. That might be easier, but it would be truly cowardly. The Spirit leads where She will and She does so with a "still small voice." We must not think we can control this. We must listen, struggle, learn, follow, argue, compromise, all in the understanding that we are not quite in charge. There is no one and nothing on the planet in our time and space, which can or should replace our absolute dependence on the Ephemeral and ever-changing constant who loves us, and *in illo tempore*, in certain times, speaks the will of God for us.

And so?

So, we are again in a watershed within the living Church. There are movements to quell any surge in lay control of funds or policies. There is a markedly evident resurgence of young order-seeking men who understand that the good of the People of God depends on their making sure that everything goes according to the rules. This seems to be in accord with a world-wide need for some sense of order in our political, economic, and moral lives. There is a felt need for order and a sense of decorum and responsibility.

On the other hand, there was a great move in the Church decades ago to empower women and men of intelligence, wit, and prayer who are not ordained. It cannot be that order only prevails if celibate men are in charge, can it? At any rate, the call to an open mind and an empathetic heart seems to be at the very heart of Christianity. It is our oldest tradition that Jesus Christ was a counter-cultural, independent thinker who loved the Law and the Temple, but who loved kindness and God's little ones more.

It is necessary that those who are ordained according to the Order of Melchizedek and who are *entitled* as members of the Order of Aaron see both sources of their call to serve as priest coming, somehow foremost, from God. It is necessary, too, that Christ's self-emptying model be the constant ideal for which we strive in all our dealings in service of the Faith and in the promotion of justice. In presiding over sacraments, we must be like Jesus, and in the private seeking after God's will in our meditation and action, we must seek His path. In other words: act with justice, love with tenderness, and walk humbly with our God. (*Micah* 6)

Why necessary? Well, if we mess up as did the leaders of Judah and Israel, we may hear like prophecy to *Jeremiah* 23 when YHWH condemns the leaders, the shepherds whom He will remove. God is biblically capable of retributive and redistributive justice. We should, actually, be afraid of getting it so wrong.

Back to Sr. Joan

What about the role of women in the ritual life of the Church? What about the laity in general in the prayer life and governance of the Church and its mission of service? Is there a significant difference between the two? Should lay men and women have more say over how the Church does her praying?——or should we return to that non-existent blissful era when the priests were in charge and all was right with the world? It does seem that there is a present movement in the world to establish religion in many states. Ayatollahs, lamas, mullahs, rabbis, bishops, priests, popes, and anointed royals are rising all over the globe. The way of the world must include seeking ways to protect the peace, to provide and preserve the rule of law. The way of the religious leaders must include thoughts about how to achieve such a reign of wisdom, to mimic God's Kingdom on the earth. But the difference between the rules of the rituals and the role of the righteousness One, as self-emptying model of the essence of priesthood, is of paramount importance. The priest, ordained to serve both God and the People of God, must have clarity within his own mind and heart. The self-emptying model, the Good Shepherd, who spent body and blood to feed His sheep, must be kept before the eyes and the soul of any who would be ordained according to the Order of Melchizedek. Otherwise, the fear expressed by both Sr. Joan and Archbishop Weakland, that the clerical cast is reasserting its hegemony over both the *presbyterium* and the Roman Church herself will have become prophecy and the downfall of the expressed will of God (expressed through the voice of the Holy Spirit breathing wind into the Council chambers only so short a time ago).

There must be prayer and attention. There must be order and ritual. There must be freedom and adherence to the *magisterium*. The priest must be humble enough to recognize that his ordering of things is only momentary and, in the grand scheme of things, a nothingness placed before the throne of the One who is. "I am; you are not," as the Lord told Catherine in her deep encounter and allowed this woman to lead a pope back to Rome while remaining herself a virtual outsider to the convent of the Dominicans. A non-priest in the strict order, she became a doctor of the Church. There is a way that we recognize quite articulately that this conundrum is normative—that the one Priest, the High Priest, Christ Jesus IS, while we are not—and yet we must do His work. Because we have been called in time and space to be *alteri Christi*, other Christs, we must be what we are not. By Grace alone are we accomplished at it.

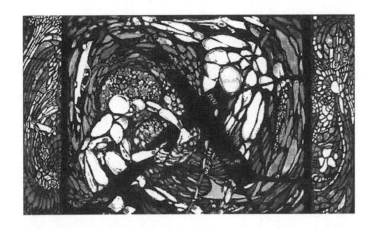

The Cover

The cover illustration is a plan for a stained glass window, part of which has been actualized at Manresa Hall, the Province Infirmary for the Jesuits of the Maryland Province of the Society of Jesus. It illustrates the central meditations of the *Spiritual Exercises* of St. Ignatius Loyola. It is included here because it depicts the evolution in the process of choice, which Ignatius recognizes as central to a follower of Christ.

Reading the window from the left, the first vertical image (in actuality eight feet by two feet) represents the *Principle and Foundation*, the meditation wherein the person making the *Exercises* becomes aware of the principle that all is gift, not necessarily good or bad, but gift. The image includes wheat and grapes, two hands holding a globe of the earth from which rises a crucified Christ. All is given. Now what do I do?

The middle window represents the choice between two goods, represented in the meditation on two earthly princes; both are appealing—one represents Christ, the other Satan. Each has a *standard* on which is represented the values of the commander. The one has plenty, power, and prestige, offered as successive goals or rewards for the followers of Satan (as in the temptation of Christ in the desert). Not bad in themselves, these are gifts, but seen as ends, they become pitfalls wherein a human may lose him/herself to the dark side. The other *standard* is the cross of Christ; He offers poverty, powerlessness, and humiliation to those who would fight in His name. The window contains a yellow Satan with a green banner, bearing images of the three stages of offering: a bag of gold coins, guns, and a parade car (money, power, pride). Satan is wrestling with a white Christ who brandishes a bloody black cross. The yin and yang are backdrop to the wrestlers, representing the consummate reality of *choice between goods* by which we become human. In the *Exercises* Ignatius recommends that we consider the principle of the MORE, the *magis,* as a guiding precept for all choices. He says a good person would choose what is better or *more conducive to the greater glory of God,* rather than following one's own untempered desires.

The third window represents the final giving back of the grateful creature. There is a priest figure in white lifting a city within a violet beehive, the New Jerusalem. The cloak of the priest contains a chalice and a broken loaf, representing the Mass, wherein the gift of each of us is joined to the gift of Christ's salvific offering.

So the image represents the depth of what one must choose every time one has to make a choice. The Church is presently in the midst of making choices about the role of the priest and the place of the ritual in her life. There is a yin and yang in the two images, types of priesthood, that of Aaron and that of Melchizedek. Let us pray that we make the better choices. All is gift. Now, what do we do?

The Author

Dennis McNally, S.J., is a painter and Professor of Fine Arts at Saint Joseph's University in Philadelphia. He has taught at Saint Joseph's for 35 years and has served as chair of the department of Fine and Performing Arts numerous times. He has earned degrees in history, fine arts, philosophy, and divinity from Fordham University, New York University and Weston Jesuit School of Theology.

A Jesuit priest, he entered the Society in 1964 and was ordained in 1974. He has been active in campus ministry, living in student housing as a resident advisor at Saint Joseph's University for almost three decades. He has also directed hundreds of spiritual seekers through the *Spiritual Exercises* of Ignatius Loyola.

His first two books, published by Wyndham Hall Press, are *Sacred Space: An Aesthetic for the Liturgical Environment* (1985) and *Fearsome Edifice: A History of the DOMUS in Catholic Churches* (2003). Both books are concerned with the architecture which houses mystery, environmental spaces which help people feel open to the divine. His recently published book, *Art for Church: Cloth of Gold, Cloak of Lead* (2010), University Press of America, carries on his examination of the relationship between the creative artist and an authoritarian church.

His painting is concerned particularly with the experience of the mystery itself. Certain themes weave themselves through his half-century of painting: What does God look like? Is there life after death? How does the Trinity relate to itself? Does Jesus have anything to add to the atrocities we live with? How does the institutional Church behave in the face of the enormous questions challenging humankind? What does God think about me? What do I think of Buddhism, the Church, Africa, the constancy of war, greed, and poverty? If his painting has a purpose, it is to say that God is involved in all the things we most deeply desire, urging us on, calling us forward, to make something beautiful of our lives.

87309542R00100

Made in the USA
Columbia, SC
12 January 2018